Gays & Guns

The Case against Homosexuals in the Military

GAYS
&
GUNS

The Case against Homosexuals in the Military

BY

JOHN A. EIDSMOE
LT. COLONEL, USAFR

WITH CONTRIBUTIONS BY

CHARLES H. DAVIS, IV
DEAN OF ACADEMIC AFFAIRS
AIR WAR COLLEGE

HUNTINGTON HOUSE PUBLISHERS

Copyright © 1993
All rights reserved. No part of this book may be
reproduced without permission from the publisher,
except by a reviewer who may quote brief passages
in a review; nor may any part of this book be
reproduced, stored in a retrieval system or copied
by mechanical photocopying, recording or other
means, without permission from the publisher.

Huntington House Publishers
P.O. Box   53788
Lafayette, Louisiana   70505

Library of Congress Card Catalog Number
Trade Paper 93-77766
Trade Paper ISBN 1-56384-043-X
Hard Cover ISBN 1-56384-046-4

Dedication

This book is respectfully dedicated

To the Glory of God;

To the millions of American men and women who have served their country in the armed forces in war and peace;

To the U.S. Air Force Academy where I have enjoyed some of my most rewarding teaching experiences;

and

To the faculty and staff of the Air War College of the Air Force, who provided valuable assistance in the writing of this book.

Contents

Contents

Disclaimer

This research report represents the views of the author and does not necessarily reflect the official opinion of the Air War College or the Department of the Air Force.

Introduction

Lifting the ban on homosexuals in the armed forces may well be the foremost issue facing America today. For it merges two vital concerns: moral values and national defense.

The economy is a relative matter. As time unfolds, prosperity and recession, inflation and deflation will come and go; interest and unemployment rates will rise and fall. Treaties and alliances will be covenanted and broken.

But the moral values the nation professes and lives by, or professes and doesn't live by, or once professed but has abandoned, endure forever. As General Douglas MacArthur observed,

> History fails to record a single precedent in which nations subject to moral decay have not passed into political and economic decline. There has been either a spiritual awakening to overcome the moral lapse, or a progressive deterioration leading to ultimate national disaster.[1]

Americans face moral upheavals and culture wars on many fronts, but few are as gut-wrenching as the issue of homosexuality. Many who have become hardened and impervious to every other practice that offends traditional morality, still feel their blood pressure rise when homosexuality is mentioned. Perhaps the reason is that, as David Horowitz explains,

[Homosexual] revolution is thus the ultimate subversive project: it proclaims the death not only of
Society's God, but also of Nature's Law—the very
idea of a reality beyond human will. For these
revolutionaries, not even biology grounds possibility or can limit human hope. Theirs is the consum-
mate Nietzchean fantasy: a world in which humanity is God. On this brave new horizon, humanity
will realize its potential as a self-creating species
able to defy its own sexual gravity.[2]

Is Horowitz exaggerating? Is this the driving force
behind the gay rights movement? The reader may answer
that question based on the evidence. It seems plain,
however, that such polarizing terms as "homophile" and
"homophobe" are not helpful in discussing the issue.
One may disapprove of homosexual acts for moral or
health reasons without hating or fearing homosexuals
as persons. As Major R. D. Adair and Captain Joseph
C. Meyers write,

. . . we live in an age of increasing intolerance in
American politics. It is an age of rhetorical excess,
which recalls the totalitarian penchant for linguistic
polarization which some have likened to verbal
terrorism. In the issue at hand, opposition to recognition of homosexuality as a constitutionally
protected classification is automatically termed
"homophobia." This is a favorite media shibboleth,
though etymologically inaccurate. A phobia is "an
abnormal or illogical fear of a specific thing or
situation." To attack someone's mental state as
"phobic" simply because he has a moral reservation
or opposing view is not unlike the approach used
in the old Soviet Union where dissidents were
diagnosed as requiring psychological treatment and
placed in "mental hospitals." The two approaches
are closely related: one who disagrees with proposed

policy changes is ridiculed as having a mental disorder.[3]

Battles may be waged over constitutional initiatives in Colorado, job discrimination against homosexuals, or legitimization of homosexual marriages. But service in the armed forces—the opportunity to enlist, train, fight, bleed, and die in the world's foremost fighting force— is the ultimate badge of legitimacy. With it come jobs, education benefits, indoctrination of military personnel in the acceptance of "alternative life-styles," and the awesome power of the federal government behind the cause of gay rights. Lifting the gay ban is not simply neutrality toward homosexuality. It is positive affirmation of the orientation and conduct by which homosexuals define themselves as a class. Against this formidable federal power, gay activists believe, state and local barriers will swiftly crumble.

Lifting the gay ban intertwines the moral issue of homosexuality with the crucial issue of defense. Our very existence as a nation, together with all its blessings, depends on a strong national defense. And for millions of veterans and their families, the old squadron, garrison, or ship evokes pungent memories, mixed but mostly fond. Would the platoon have been as combat-ready if it had contained open gays?

No wonder the issue of gays in the military evokes such profound emotions! It merges two of the nation's most vital concerns—moral values and national defense.

This book will demonstrate that the opposition to homosexuals in the military is more than irrational fear or "phobia." Besides legitimate religious and moral values, the opposition is based upon sound medical and scientific evidence that the homosexual life-style poses many physical and mental health hazards, upon legitimate concerns for heterosexual privacy, and upon the considered opinion of military experts that the presence of homosexuals in combat units has the effect of polarizing those combat units and undermining morale and discipline.

The book will examine the nature and extent of homosexuality, current military policy, and the moral, legal, hygienic, social, economic, and other issues concerning homosexuality and the military. Because the author's own military experience has been in the Air Force, the book frequently uses Air Force regulations as examples; however, the issues addressed should be relevant to all branches of the armed forces.

The author hopes the substantive facts and ideas presented in this book will make a positive contribution to the discussion and resolution of this issue.

1

What is Homosexuality?

Definitions

Air Force Regulation 36-2(C3), para. 1-10(c), defines "homosexual" as "a person, regardless of sex, who engages in, or desires to engage in, or intends to engage in homosexual acts." Paragraph 1-10(d) defines "homosexual acts" as "bodily contact, actively undertaken or passively permitted, between members of the same sex for the purpose of satisfying sexual desires." As explained later, Air Force regulations 36-2 (for officers) and 39-10 (for enlisted personnel) distinguish between homosexual tendencies (erotic desire for a member of one's own sex even if such desire never results in overt acts) and homosexual acts; both are unacceptable, but homosexual acts can result in more severe consequences than homosexual tendencies without homosexual acts.

These definitions seem consistent with *Webster's Collegiate Dictionary, Fifth Edition,* which defines "homosexuality" as "eroticism for one of the same sex," and *The Random House Dictionary of the English Language, Unabridged 1967 Edition,* which defines "homosexuality" as "sexual desire or behavior directed toward a person or persons of one's own sex."

Some believe heterosexuality and homosexuality should not be viewed as black and white absolutes. Some people, it is argued, are exclusively attracted to members of the opposite sex (heterosexuals), and some are exclusively attracted to members of their own sex (homosexuals). In between are bisexuals, those who are attracted to both sexes. And most people, according to this argument, do not fit neatly into one of these three categories. Rather, heterosexuality and homosexuality must be viewed as a continuum. A person might be exclusively heterosexual, primarily heterosexual, bisexual, primarily homosexual, or exclusively homosexual; or he might be considered 90 percent heterosexual and 10 percent homosexual, or 30 percent heterosexual and 70 percent homosexual.[1]

For the sake of clarity, unless otherwise noted, the term "gay" will refer to male homosexuality, "lesbian" will refer to female homosexuality, and "homosexual" will refer to homosexuality of either or both sexes.

Extent of Homosexuality

The debate over the extent of homosexuality is more than academic; it goes to the very heart of the drive of gay rights advocates for full legal recognition. Their orientation and conduct cannot be abnormal, they insist, if a large percentage of the population is homosexual. Furthermore, the larger their numbers, the more manpower the military is losing by not accepting homosexuals. The percentage is also highly relevant in considering the extent to which homosexuals are a disproportionate risk of contracting and spreading AIDS and other diseases. It also affects the credibility of the Kinsey Report itself.

Since Dr. Alfred C. Kinsey and his associates produced *Sexual Behavior in the Human Male* in 1948 and *Sexual Behavior in the Human Female* in 1953, commentators have frequently echoed the conclusion that roughly 10 percent of the population of the United States is homosexual. That is an oversimplification of Dr. Kinsey's conclusions. Actually Dr. Kinsey concluded that:

> 37 percent of the total male population has at least some overt homosexual experience to the point of orgasm between adolescence and old age. . . .

> 13 percent of the [male] population has more of the homosexual than the heterosexual for at least three years between the age of 16 and 55. . . .

> 10 percent of the males are more or less exclusively homosexual for at least three years between the ages of 16 and 55. . . .

> 8 percent of the males are exclusively homosexual for at least three years between the ages of 16 and 55. . . .

> 4 percent of the white males are exclusively homosexual throughout their lives, after the onset of adolescence.[2]

In _Sexual Behavior in the Human Female_, Kinsey and his associates concluded that the incidence of female homosexuality was much less than that of male homosexuality. Thirteen percent of females had experienced homosexual activity to the point of orgasm compared to 37 percent of males, and only about half to a third as many females were primarily or exclusively homosexual.[3]

It follows the old adage that if something is stated often enough, the public will eventually accept the message without argument, no matter how outrageous— or unsubstantiated—it may be. Though the claim is that Kinsey said 10 percent of the population is homosexual, this is misleading. If 4 percent of adult males are exclusively homosexual and the percentage among adult females is half that of males or less (2 percent), then Kinsey really said the actual percentage of adults who are exclusively homosexual throughout their lives is 3 percent or less.

But beyond the misrepresentation of Kinsey's conclusions is a more sinister specter, because even Kinsey's figures may be greatly inflated due to faulty research methods. Dr. Judith A. Reisman and associates, in their book *Kinsey, Sex and Fraud*, criticize Kinsey's research for several reasons:

- The subjects of their study, while extensive in number, included only volunteers. At the time Kinsey's studies were underway, the eminent psychiatrist Dr. Abraham Mazlow repeatedly warned Kinsey that a study group composed of volunteers would not be representative of society as a whole, particularly on sexual matters, because the typical person is reluctant to talk about such matters; but Kinsey ignored Mazlow's warning.[4]

- About one-fourth of Kinsey's male volunteers were prisoners in penal institutions, in many cases having been convicted of sex offenses. Their responses are not likely to be representative of society as a whole.[5]

- Kinsey initially included substantial numbers of prisoners and nonwhites in his female study, and then excluded them from his conclusions for reasons that are unclear.[6]

- Kinsey and associates conducted experiments on children, including forced stimulation of their genitals, in ways that could constitute criminal child sexual abuse.[7]

- Kinsey and his associates appear to have had a predisposition toward considering homosexuality, bestiality, incest, pedophilia, and other sexual practices

as "normal," and slanted the study toward that conclusion. For example, Kinsey's interviewers often
assumed participants had engaged certain sexual
practices and would ask when the person began the
practice, not whether he or she engaged in the
practice.[8]

Despite this distortion and flawed methodology, this
misleading figure of 10 percent is commonly cited
authoritatively today. And in this writer's opinion this
is often not an innocent mistake. The public is being
led to believe it is an accurate figure. It is part of a
deliberate attempt to gain the public's acceptance of
homosexuality as "normal" by telling them it is more
common than it really is.

However, more recent research indicates that the
actual number of homosexuals in American society is
considerably lower than Dr. Kinsey estimated:

- In 1989 a study of 36,741 Minnesota teen-agers
  concluded that only 1.5 percent of the males and
  1.1 percent of the females were homosexual or
  bisexual.[9]
- The National Science Foundation funded a study
  released by the National Opinion Research Center
  in 1991. Surveying only sexually active adults, the
  study found that only 2 percent had been bisexual
  or exclusively homosexual during the preceding year,
  and only 5 to 6 percent had been bisexual or exclusively homosexual since age eighteen. Again, this
  study was limited to sexually active adults; had it
  included the entire population, the figure would have
  been much lower.[10]
- In 1989 the *British Medical Journal* reported a study
  of randomly selected British males which revealed
  that just under 3 percent were engaged in homosexual activity.[11]

- Other evidence, such as patronage of gay bookstores, gay bars, gay rallies, membership in gay organizations, etc., would indicate the homosexual population to be a tiny fraction of the oft-quoted 10 percent figure.[12]

- Congressman William E. Dannemeyer (R-CA), in testimony before a Republican Research Committee hearing on 9 December 1992 stated:

  Of the twenty-some odd studies ever conducted to measure the extent of persons claiming exclusive homosexuality, none come even close to ten percent. Most are one to three percent. Only Kinsey breaks three percent, and he goes no higher than eight notwithstanding that most persons he interviewed were white male sex offenders in prison, university students, and patrons of homosexual bars.[13]

Because of the faulty methodology used in the Kinsey study and its inconsistency with many more recent studies, it seems likely that the actual homosexual population in the United States is substantially lower than the oft-quoted 10 percent. A figure of 2 percent would be more realistic—one-fifth, 20 percent of the more impressive and threatening numbers pressed on the public by Kinsey and his disciples in the media, higher education, the medical field, legal circles, and liberal politicians and their special interest groups.

Is the percentage of homosexuals in the armed forces comparable to that in American society as a whole? Many writers assume it is, but in plain fact no one knows for sure because homosexuals in the military usually do not admit their orientation. The Department of Defense, in its response to the June 1992 Report of the General Accounting Office (GAO), speculated that the number of homosexuals in the armed forces may in fact be significantly lower than that of the general population because homosexuals, knowing the military policy on homosexuality, tend to stay away from military service.[14]

Mary Ann Humphrey, who in 1987 resigned from the Army in lieu of discharge proceedings for homosexuality, edited a book entitled *My Country, My Right to Serve, Experiences of Gay Men and Women in the Military, World War II to the Present* (New York: Harper Collins, 1990), in which about forty-one homosexuals recount their personal experiences in the armed forces. These accounts may be helpful in understanding the human dilemma homosexuals face; however, they provide no empirical data on which to base overall conclusions or casually dropped blanket statements broadcast on the evening news. My personal conversations with present and former Air Force Academy cadets, faculty, and staff indicate that homosexual acts are extremely rare at the Academy.

Since homosexuals constitute no more than 2 percent of the general population and the DOD exclusion policy in all likelihood has some deterrent effect upon enlistment, I can draw no other conclusion than that the percentage of practicing homosexuals in the armed forces is less than 2 percent of the total force.

Is Homosexuality "Abnormal"?

The debate over numbers is more than academic; for homosexuals, it is the lynchpin of the gay rights drive for affirmation and legal status. Homosexuality, it is argued, cannot be an "abnormality" if a large portion of the population practices it and does not seem abnormal in other respects. (Note, however, that if the biblical account is to be believed, God destroyed the cities of Sodom and Gomorrah because of their sodomite practices, even though almost the entire population engaged in sodomy [Genesis 18-19].) The larger the homosexual population is perceived to be, the more political and economic clout it wields, and the more potential manpower and talent the armed forces are losing by refusing to admit them into the armed forces.

Sigmund Freud was ambivalent toward homosexuality; he considered it an "arrest of sexual development" because heterosexual sex is the natural objective of the sex drive, but he also said it was "nothing to be ashamed of" and not an "illness."[15] Recently the mental health profession has moved toward greater acceptance of homosexuality. In 1973 the American Psychiatric Association removed it from its list of mental illnesses, concluding that "homosexuality per se implies no impairment in judgment, stability, reliability, or general, social or vocational capabilities."[16] The American Psychological Association followed suit two years later by adopting a similar position in 1975.[17] The significant victory gained by the homosexual lobby as a result of these actions strikes at the heart of American life. The ramifications include the countless day-to-day legal and medical decisions that are made based upon these criteria—decisions that often affect funding and disbursements of monies.

Some mental health professionals do not agree with the positions taken by the American Psychiatric Association and the American Psychological Association. Among those taking a different position are New York psychotherapist Edward W. Eichel, Dr. Paul Cameron of the Family Research Institute, and Dr. Frank du Mas, chairman of the Department of Psychology at Augusta College, Georgia.

Ultimately one's view of homosexuality depends

largely upon one's view of God and His laws, of the nature of man, and of basic morals and values. Theologians, scholars, ethicists, and philosophers continuously debate the veracity of the literature addressing the normalcy of the homosexual life-style, notwithstanding the definitive condemnation unequivocally articulated by God Himself in the Bible. These are questions to which psychiatry does not necessarily have the final answers.

Nevertheless, solid factual reasons exist—undisputed but largely ignored in most of the well-publicized current literature on the subject—by which one might conclude that homosexuality, regardless of whether it is "normal" or "abnormal," involves highly unusual behavior. For example:

Practicing homosexuals generally engage in homosexual activity with a large number of partners. This has been recognized even by researchers for the Kinsey Institute. In 1978 Alan P. Bell and Martin S. Weinberg, researching for the Kinsey Institute, reported that the average practicing homosexual had more than 250 partners during his lifetime; 43 percent claimed to have had sex with five hundred or more partners; and almost 30 percent reported having one thousand or more partners.[18] In *Sexually Transmitted Diseases and Homosexuality* (1983), Dr. David A. Ostrow says, "The median number of lifetime sexual partners of the [more than] 4,000 [homosexual] respondents was 49.5. Many reported ranges of 300-400, and 472 individuals reported 'over 1,000' different lifetime sexual partners."[19]

Dr. Anne C. Collier, in her 1987 *American Journal of Medicine* entry, says, "The homosexual men had significantly more sexual partners in the preceding one month, six months, and lifetime (median 2, 9, and 200 partners respectively), than the heterosexual subjects (median 1, 1, and 14 partners)."[20] Dr. Mary E. Guinan, writing in the *Annals of Internal Medicine* (1984), concluded,

> Heterosexual patients from all risk groups reported considerably fewer sexual partners than did homosexual men, both for the year before onset of illness and for lifetime. In addition, sexual practices found to be frequent among homosexual men were rare among heterosexual risk groups. Few heterosexual patients were exposed to feces during sex or had rectal trauma. Only one of the interviewed heterosexual patients had a history of parasitic diarrhea.[21]

In a 1984 entry in *Medicine*, Dr. Jonathan W. M. Gold, M.D., reported that in a study of ninety-three homosexuals, the "mean number of estimated lifetime sexual partners was 1,422 (median, 377; range, 15-7000)."[22] Drs. Paul Cameron, Kirk Cameron, and Kay Proctor conducted a study of 4,340 adults and discovered that the average homosexual male had a median of one hundred sexual partners during his lifetime while the average homosexual female had four. This activity is compared to the numbers for heterosexual males and females which were eight and three respectively![23]

One might question these numbers, though it might be more prudent to consider the possibility that sexually active persons would underestimate rather than overestimate the number of partners. One possible reason for the variation in the numbers in these studies may be the age of the homosexual respondents. Obviously no respondent is able to state the total number of sexual partners during his lifetime; his life isn't over yet. Older homosexual respondents are likely to report more contacts than younger ones.

The significant point is that all of these studies come

to the same conclusion: *Practicing homosexuals have many times more partners than heterosexuals do.* As will be discussed in chapter 5, this factor highlights potential health ramifications which must be considered in deciding whether admitting homosexuals is truly in the best interest of the armed forces.

The essence of the normalcy of homosexuality may be analyzed best when exposing the unusualness of its behaviors. Besides having far more sex partners, practicing homosexuals are much more likely to engage in sexual practices that many would characterize as vile or immoral or both. In their above-cited study, Drs. Cameron, Cameron, and Proctor found that 37 percent of gay males practice sadomasochism; 32 percent engage in bondage (tying up or being tied up by their partners); 42 percent place their fists in their partners' anuses (called "fisting" or "handballing"); 29 percent urinate on their partners or are urinated upon by them (called "golden showers"); 17 percent practiced defecation with their partners (called "scat"); 15 percent have had sex with animals; 34 percent have paid for sex; 88 percent have engaged in orgies, group sex, or sex with threesomes; 68 percent have had sex in gay baths; 50 percent have had sex in peep shows or booths; and 66 percent have had sex in public restrooms.

Homosexual males were 6.6 times more likely than heterosexual males to engage in sadomasochism; 2.9 times more likely to practice bondage; 18.8 times more likely to engage in "handballing"; 5.8 times more likely to practice "golden showers"; 10.1 times more likely to engage in "scat"; 6.4 times more likely to engage in sex with animals; 3.4 times more likely to engage in sex with threesomes, orgies, or group sex; 57.6 times more likely to have sex in a gay bath; 13.8 times more likely to have sex in a peep show or booth; and 7.2 times more likely to have sex in a public restroom.[24]

In every category, lesbians were less likely to engage in such activity than gays, and female heterosexuals were less likely to engage in such activity than male heterosexuals. Likewise, in every category except possibly sex with animals, lesbians were more likely to engage in such activity than female heterosexuals, though in most categories the differences were not as pronounced as that between gays and male heterosexuals. The only exception involved paying for sex. Gays were slightly less likely (0.9) to pay for sex than were heterosexual men, but gays were 4.5 times more likely to be paid for sex than were heterosexual men. Lesbians were 12.8 times more likely to pay for sex, and 11.2 times more likely to be paid for sex, than were heterosexual women.[25]

Others studies have reached similar conclusions. Dr. Mary E. Guinan concluded that 98 percent of gay men but only 13 percent of heterosexual men practiced anal intercourse, while 94 percent of gay men but only 3 percent of heterosexual men were the recipients of such action.[26] And in a 1988 _Journal of the American Medical Association_ article, Dr. Walter E. Stamm, et. al., reported that "Ninety-two percent of these men [in the study] reported that they practiced receptive anal intercourse, and 63 percent practiced analingus [tongue in anus]."[27]

Not only undesirable to most people, these activities present numerous health, disease, and sanitation problems. The armed forces should rightly consider them carefully in determining whether to change the policy.

These studies do not say all or even most homosexuals engage in all of these types of behavior. They do provide convincing evidence, however, that a disproportionate number of them do.

So is homosexuality "abnormal?" What one perceives as abnormality, mental disease, or deviant behavior might vary according to one's own views and practices or one's concept of normality. But consider the following: (1) the number of practicing homosexuals appears to be much smaller than commonly reported; (2) homosexuals engage in activities that most people, both now and throughout history, consider unusual or offensive or vile; and (3) these activities could have serious adverse health consequences for those who engage in them and for others.

Clearly a rational basis exists for concluding that homosexuality is not normal. Still, the distortion of data and the outright bullying tactics of the militant gay lobby have nearly convinced the key decision-makers that this perverse practice is nothing more than a life-style—and one engaged in by an impressive (and falsely inflated) voting bloc! These lies affected for the sake of self-indulgence and self-delusion threaten the fortitude of our armed forces.

Current Department of Defense Policy on Homosexuality

With some variation in wording, rationale, and application, the United States military policy toward homosexuality has been unchanged since the continental army of General Washington. That policy is currently summarized in Department of Defense Directive 1332.14 (dated 28 January 1982 concerning enlisted personnel) and 1332.30 (dated 12 February 1986 concerning officers). These directives state:

> Homosexuality is incompatible with military service. The presence in the military environment of persons who engage in homosexual conduct or who, by their statements, demonstrate a propensity to engage in homosexual conduct, seriously impairs the accomplishment of the military mission. The presence of such members adversely affects the ability of the Military Services to maintain discipline, good order, and morale; to foster mutual trust and confidence among service members; to ensure the integrity of the system of rank and command; to facilitate assignment and worldwide deployment of service members who frequently must live and work under close conditions affording minimal privacy;

to recruit and retain members of the Military Services; to maintain public acceptability of military service; and to prevent breaches of security.

Consistent with that policy, the armed forces prohibit sodomy in Article 125 of the Uniform Code of Military Justice:

> Any person subject to this chapter who engages in unnatural carnal copulation with another person of the same or opposite sex or with an animal is guilty of sodomy. Penetration, however slight, is sufficient to complete the offense.

Occasionally Article 133 of the UCMJ, "Conduct Unbecoming an Officer and a Gentleman," and Article 134, "Conduct Prejudicial to the Good Order and Discipline of the Armed Forces," have been used to prosecute matters involving homosexuality.

The Uniform Code of Military Justice is nondiscriminatory in its application to all branches of the armed forces, to homosexual as well as heterosexual sodomy, and to males and females alike. It is adopted by Congress and can be changed only by act of Congress, subject of course to a presidential veto, which two-thirds of both houses of Congress could override.

The President cannot amend an act of Congress, so he cannot change the UCMJ without congressional action. But the authority to make regulations for the armed forces is shared by Congress and the President. According to Article II, Section 2, Clause (2) of the Constitution, the President is the "Commander in Chief of the Army and Navy of the United States, and of the Militia of the several States, when called into the actual Service of the United States." However, Article I, Section 8 provides that Congress has the power "To declare War" (Clause 11), "To raise and support Armies" (Clause 12),

"To provide and maintain a Navy" (Clause 13), "To make rules for the Government and Regulation of the land and naval Forces" (Clause 14), "To provide for calling forth the Militia to execute the Laws of the Union, suppress insurrections and repel invasions" (Clause 15), and "To provide for organizing, arming, and disciplining, the Militia, and for governing such Part of them as may be employed in the Service of the United States, reserving to the States respectively, the Appointment of the Officers, and the Authority of training the Militia according to the discipline imposed by Congress" (Clause 16).

As commander in chief of the armed forces, the President apparently has authority to adopt certain policies and regulations concerning the armed forces. However, Art. I, Sec. 8, Cl. (14) makes clear that the final authority to make rules or regulations for the government and regulation of the armed forces rests with Congress. If Congress were to enact a law codifying the DOD policy or individual service regulations on homosexuality, the President would not have the power to change or nullify that law. He possibly could veto it, though such action would be subject to being overridden by Congress.

The President's authority over the National Guard is less clear, since the Guard traditionally is under state control (e.g., Wyoming National Guard, etc.). The President is commander in chief of the Guard when the Guard is in federal service, but Congress retains final authority to call the Guard into federal service. The states train the Guard and appoint officers for the Guard when the Guard is not in federal service. All direction is nonetheless subject to the discipline prescribed by Congress; but the Constitution nowhere gives the President authority over the Guard when the Guard is not in federal service. Taking these restrictions into account, whether the President could impose regulations upon the Guard while the Guard is not in federal service is a serious constitutional question. If the President ordered the admission of homosexuals into the National Guard, and a governor responded "Not in the Guard in my state!"—the result could be a landmark case.

The regulations of the various services repeat the basic policy established in the DOD directive. For example, Air Force Regulation 36-2 covers the administrative discharge of officers, and AFR 39-10 covers the administrative discharge of enlisted personnel. AFR 36-2 begins by saying in paragraph 1-1,

> Continued service as an officer is a privilege that may be terminated when such action is determined to be in the best interest of the Air Force.

Chapter 2 of AFR 36-2 provides for the discharge of officers because of "substandard performance of duty" and includes substandard performance because of "character and behavior disorders." Character and behavior disorders include, in para. 2-3(g)(5), "Psychological disorders excluding homosexuality and psychosexual disorders." Homosexuality is specifically excluded under chapter 2 because it is covered in chapter 3 of AFR 36-2 instead.

Chapter 3, entitled "Misconduct, Moral or Professional Dereliction, or in the Interest of National Security," does include homosexuality. Para. 3-7 specifically lists homosexuality as a basis for discharge under this section and refers to para. 3-4 for specifics. Para. 3-4(a) recites the DOD directive verbatim. Para. 3-4(b) declares that regardless of when in the individual's life the conduct occurred or the statements were made—prior to or during military service—the member will be discharged if any of the following activities are conclusively found to have taken place:

> (1) The member has engaged in, attempted to engage in, or solicited another to engage in a homosexual act or acts unless [here follows an exceptional circumstance that will be discussed later] . . .
>
> (2) The member has stated that he or she is a homosexual or bisexual unless there is a further finding that he is not a homosexual or bisexual.
>
> (3) The member has married or attempted to marry a person known to be the same biological sex (as evidenced by the external anatomy of the persons involved) unless there are further findings that the member is not a homosexual or bisexual and that the purpose of the marriage or attempt was the avoidance or termination of military service.

Subparagraph (1) above provides for exceptional circumstances in which an officer who has engaged in or attempted to engage in or solicited homosexual acts may nevertheless be retained in military service. According to subparagraph (1), those circumstances which will except such persons from discharge are:

> (a) Such conduct is a departure from the member's usual and customary behavior; and
>
> (b) Such conduct under all the circumstances is unlikely to recur; and
>
> (c) Such conduct was not accomplished by use of force, coercion, or intimidation by the member during a period of military service; and
>
> (d) Under the particular circumstances of the case, the member's continued presence in the Service is consistent with the interest of the Service in proper good discipline, good order, and morale; and

(e) The member does not desire to engage in or intend to engage in homosexual acts.

Paragraph 3-2 of AFR 36-2 provides that an officer discharged for misconduct under Paragraph 3 (the paragraph which, among other things, covers homosexuality)

> will, as a rule, be discharged under other than honorable conditions unless the Secretary of the Air Force determines the officer according to AFR 36-12, paragraph 1-6, (1) should be honorably discharged, or (2) should receive a general (under honorable conditions) discharge.

Paragraph 3-2 further provides in subparagraph (d):

> When homosexuality is the sole basis for discharge, an honorable or general (under honorable conditions) discharge will, as a rule, be issued. A characterization of under other than honorable conditions discharge may be issued if there is a finding that the officer attempted, solicited, or committed a homosexual act:
>
> (1) By using force, coercion, or intimidation;
>
> (2) With a person under 16 years of age;
>
> (3) With a subordinate in circumstances that violate customary military superior and subordinate relationship (The subordinate and the superior do not have to be in the same chain of command.);
>
> (4) Openly in public view;
>
> (5) For compensation;
>
> (6) Aboard a military vessel or aircraft; or
>
> (7) In another location subject to military control under aggravating circumstances, noted in the finding, that have an adverse impact on discipline, good order, or morale comparable to the impact of such activity aboard a vessel or aircraft.

Addressing enlisted personnel, Air Force Regulation 39-10 contains similar language and provisions for the discharge of those who have admitted to being homosexual or who have been found to engage in, attempted to engage in, or solicited homosexual acts. The regulations of the Army, Navy, Marines, and Coast Guard are similar to those of the Air Force.

Between 1980 and 1990, 16,919 persons were officially discharged for homosexuality. The number discharged each year between 1980 and 1990 declined about 47 percent, and this decline was reflected in all branches of the armed forces. During the same period, involuntary discharges of all types for any reason declined by about 36 percent. In keeping with involuntary discharges generally, by 1990 discharges for homosexuality were more likely to be characterized as honorable or general, whereas in 1980 and before they were more likely to be characterized as undesirable (enlisted) or other than honorable (officers). Certainly gay rights advocates cannot read harshness into this evolution of classification of the discharges. In proportion to the total force, discharges for homosexuality were more frequent in the Navy and Marines than in the Air Force and Army, possibly reflecting the unique conditions of Navy and Marine duty (extended cruises, special operations, etc.).

For some reason, women are more likely to be discharged for homosexuality than men, even though women in general are less likely than men to be homosexual. Whites are more likely than nonwhites to be discharged for homosexuality.[1]

In this day of militant gay activists demanding lifting of the ban, what does the public think about the policy? Does military policy concerning homosexuals reflect current public opinion? The 1992 GAO report cited a series of Gallup polls in which the percentage of people supporting the admission of homosexuals into the armed forces steadily increased from 51 percent in 1977 to 52 percent in 1980, 55 percent in 1985 and 1987, 60 percent in 1989, and 69 percent in 1991.[2] More recent studies indicate the percentage favoring admission of homosexuals has shrunk considerably, and that today the public is about evenly divided on the subject. A late 1992 study by the Associated Press showed that 46 percent of the public support admission, 44 percent oppose admission, and 10 percent are undecided. However, present and former military personnel strongly oppose admission of homosexuals; a Gallup poll of the members of the Retired Officers Association showed 83 percent against the change.[3] And perhaps most significant, the outpouring of opposition that overwhelmed Congress and the White House in January 1993 indicates that the poll percentages do not tell the full story; the opposition is much more intense than many believed.

Poll results can vary greatly depending upon how the questions are worded. One might simply ask, "Should military personnel be discriminated against because of sexual orientation?" and receive a very negative response. Americans are personal freedom-oriented, and the very term "discrimination" triggers a predictable reaction. In this case, "No." But if the same people were asked, "Should your son or daughter be forced to sleep, shower, and serve in the trenches with homosexuals?"—the answers would likely be very different.

One thing is obvious: Despite what the evening news anchors tell you, there is no clear consensus that current military policy on homosexuality should be changed.

3

A Response to Arguments for Lifting the Gay Ban

Those who believe homosexuals should be allowed into the armed forces present their arguments in many forms. But essentially their arguments boil down to three: (1) Homosexuals have a right to serve in the armed forces without discrimination; (2) The ban is unenforceable since homosexuals serve "under cover" anyway; and (3) The ban deprives the armed forces of a valuable manpower resource. These arguments have received a great deal of media attention, and each needs to be examined closely. Let us address them in order. While it will be apparent that I oppose admitting homosexuals into the armed forces, I hope and believe this section constitutes a fair and objective consideration of the arguments of those who advocate otherwise.

(1) *Homosexuals have a right to serve in the armed forces without discrimination.*

Homosexuals, it is argued, are human beings just like everyone else except for their sexual orientation. They should therefore have the same rights as others, including military service. The struggle for gay rights today is comparable to the struggle for civil rights for blacks in the 1950s and 1960s and the struggle for equal rights for women in the 1970s. And, time is on their side. Eventually, homosexuals will win their struggle for acceptance; the only question is when. Unless the armed forces voluntarily change their repressive and outmoded policies, the courts will force them to do so, just as the courts forced the South to integrate forty years ago.

In _My Country, My Right to Serve_, Mary Ann Humphries declares that military service is "my constitutional right."[1] In fact, her premise, like the second half of her title, is flawed. Military service has never been regarded as a constitutional right. Serving in the armed forces is a privilege, which the government may grant or withhold, and sometimes a duty, which may be required, but not a right that the citizen can claim as absolute. The privilege may be terminated when the best interest of the military and the best interest of the nation so require. Many long-term soldiers are discovering this today as reductions in force go into effect.

However, some constitutional protections do apply. For example, the equal protection clause of the Fourteenth Amendment ("nor shall any State . . . deny to any person within its jurisdiction the equal protection of the laws") has been applied, at least in principle, to the federal government in _Bolling v. Sharpe_ (1954)[2] by virtue of the Fifth Amendment protection against being deprived of "life, liberty or property, without due process of law."

But the Fourteenth Amendment does not prohibit all forms of discrimination. It only prohibits discrimination that lacks a sound basis. For example, nothing in the Fourteenth Amendment prohibits a state law school from admitting students who make high marks on the Law School Admission Test while rejecting those who make low scores, because it is reasonable to conclude that applicants who do well on the LSAT will do better in law school, and become better lawyers, than those who do not. Similarly, nothing in the Constitution prohibits the Air Force from accepting top-notch law graduates into the Judge Advocate General Corps while rejecting those who graduated at the bottom of their classes; once again, the Air Force has good reason to believe that, in general, top law students will be better JAGs.

So the Constitution does not forbid all discrimination, only unjust discrimination. And what is "unjust" discrimination? The courts analyze different categories of discrimination in different ways.

Generally speaking, unjust discrimination is that discrimination which lacks a rational basis. It is rational and sensible to discriminate in some ways. It is rational for the Judge Advocate General to prefer law school graduates with high grade point averages over those with low GPAs. It is rational for the Air Force to prefer pilots with good vision over those who have poor vision. The armed forces discriminate by refusing to enlist quadriplegics, blind and deaf persons, alcoholics, persons with mental disorders, those who are mentally retarded, amputees, and many other categories. The armed forces can and should discriminate in these categories because a rational basis for such discrimination exists; there is good reason to believe persons who fall into those categories could hinder the mission of the armed forces.

For some types of discrimination, particularly racial discrimination, more than a rational basis is necessary. If the discrimination involves a "suspect classification" or the denial of a "fundamental right," the courts apply a standard of "strict scrutiny," analyzing whether the government has a compelling interest that cannot be achieved by less restrictive means. Enter here the game

of "compelling interest one-upmanship," when opposing sides claim a monopoly on perceiving whether the
government has a compelling interest to act in a restrictive way that results in a form of discrimination. In
truth, there are often as many methods of analyzing and
applying the compelling interest rule as there are judges
on the bench.

Racial discrimination is a "suspect classification,"
because no legitimate reason for racial discrimination
exists, and throughout American history and that of
other nations, racial discrimination has been practiced
arbitrarily, unfairly, and maliciously.

The case law establishes that discrimination based
upon sexual orientation does not fit into that upper tier
"strict scrutiny" category. First, sexual orientation is not
a "suspect classification"; legitimate reasons exist for
treating homosexuals differently as will be demonstrated
in the next several chapters.

Second, homosexuality does not involve a "fundamental" constitutional right. As the Supreme Court noted
in *Bowers v. Hardwick* (1986), certain rights are considered more "fundamental" or "preferred" than others;
such rights are entitled to "heightened judicial protection." Which rights are "fundamental?" Justice White,
speaking for the 5-4 majority in *Bowers v. Hardwick*, offered the following explanation:

> Striving to assure itself and the public that announc-
> ing rights not readily identifiable in the
> Constitution's text involves much more than the
> imposition of the Justices' own choice of values on
> the States and the Federal Government, the Court
> has sought to identify the nature of the rights
> qualifying for heightened judicial protection. In *Palko
> v. Connecticut* . . . (1937), it was said that this cat-
> egory includes those fundamental liberties that are

"implicit in the concept of ordered liberty," such that "neither liberty nor justice would exist if [they] were sacrificed." A different description of fundamental liberties appeared in *Moore v. East Cleveland* ... (1977) ... where they are characterized as those liberties that are "deeply rooted in this Nation's history and tradition. . . ."

It is obvious to us that neither of these formulations would extend a fundamental right to homosexuals to engage in acts of consensual sodomy. Proscriptions against that conduct have ancient roots. . . . Sodomy was a criminal offense at common law and was forbidden by the laws of the original thirteen States when they ratified the Bill of Rights. In 1868, when the Fourteenth Amendment was ratified, all but 5 of the 37 States in the Union had criminal sodomy laws. In fact, until 1961, all 50 States outlawed sodomy, and today, 24 States and the District of Columbia continue to provide criminal penalties for sodomy performed in private and between consenting adults. . . . Against this background, to claim that a right to engage in such conduct is "deeply rooted in this Nation's history and tradition" or "implicit in the concept of ordered liberty" is, at best, facetious.[3]

As noted, *Bowers v. Hardwick* was decided in 1986 by a vote of 5-4. Since 1986, two of the dissenting justices, Brennan and Marshall, have left the Court and have been replaced by Justices Souter and Thomas, who generally vote with the Court's conservative bloc. This writer, as a constitutional attorney and professor of constitutional law as well as an Air Force Judge Advocate, believes that if a similar case were before the Court again today, the result would be the same but the vote would be 7-2 instead of 5-4.

Since homosexuality does not involve fundamental rights or suspect classifications, a state does not need to show a compelling interest that cannot be achieved by less restrictive means in order to win in court. All the state needs to demonstrate is that its policy on homosexuality has a rational basis. As following chapters demonstrate, this rational basis does indeed exist.

Furthermore, the armed forces are in a much stronger legal position on this issue than are the state governments because of the unique demands of military discipline. In *Goldman v. Weinberger* (1986), *Greer v. Spock* (1976), and many other cases, the Supreme Court has recognized that the armed forces have an interest in maintaining good order and discipline.[4] Further, when the military insists that a certain policy is necessary to maintain order and discipline, the Court generally defers to that military determination even where fundamental rights are involved—and as noted earlier, no such fundamental rights are involved here.

Despite all of the media publicity surrounding court cases, the plain fact remains that every court of final jurisdiction that has ever ruled on the armed forces' exclusion of homosexuals has upheld the basic policy as constitutional.

Several courts have struck down certain aspects of the policy or the way it was administered. For example in *Matlovich v. Secretary of the Air Force* (1978), the appeals court held that, since Air Force regulations provided that in "unusual circumstances" an airman who had engaged in homosexual behavior could be retained, TSgt. Matlovich was entitled to be informed specifically why these "unusual circumstances" did not apply to him. The case was subsequently settled out of court, and the regulation was subsequently modified.[5]

An Army case involved SSgt. Perry Watkins, who served fourteen years on active duty, acknowledged his homosexual orientation from the beginning of his career and was allowed to re-enlist on three occasions even though the Army knew of his homosexuality. Around 1982 the Army revoked his security clearance and refused to allow him to re-enlist, citing his homosexuality as the sole reason. The Ninth Circuit Court of Appeals held that the Army, by repeatedly allowing SSgt. Watkins to re-enlist, was estopped from discharging SSgt. Watkins for homosexuality because SSgt. Watkins had disclosed his orientation from the beginning and had built an Army career in justifiable reliance upon the Army's acceptance of his orientation.[6]

Again, each of these cases involves the procedures used in discharging homosexuals; none invalidates the policy itself. In *Dronenburg v. Zech* (1984), the circuit court of appeals held that there is no constitutional right to engage in homosexual conduct and upheld the Navy's policy on homosexuality as a rational means of achieving legitimate government interests such as discipline, good order, and morale. The court stated:

> The effects of homosexual conduct within a naval or military unit are almost certain to be harmful to morale and discipline. The Navy is not required to produce social science data or the results of controlled experiments to prove what common sense and common experience demonstrate.[7]

In *Ben-Shalom v. Marsh* (1990), an Army reserve case, the Seventh Circuit reached a similar result, upholding the Army's authority to discharge Sgt. Ben-Shalom for homosexuality and rejecting Sgt. Ben-Shalom's First Amendment claim that Army policy violated her right to freedom of speech because it prevented her from making statements about her sexual orientation. The court ruled that the regulation did not prohibit free speech but rather prohibited the homosexuality that Sgt. Ben-Shalom's speech identified. The court said that when speech and non-speech elements are combined in the same course of conduct, limitations on speech are permissible when there is a sufficiently important government interest involved. The court ruled further that the rational basis standard is the appropriate test in homosexuality cases, and that a rational basis for the Army's policy does exist.[8]

In still another case, _Pruitt v. Cheney_ (1991), the Ninth Circuit again held that the military policy of excluding homosexuals is to be evaluated according to a lower-tier "rational basis" test rather than an upper-tier "strict scrutiny" test or a middle-tier "substantial relationship to important governmental objectives" test. The court did note that the government's rational basis could not consist simply of stereotypes or prejudice.[9]

In constitutional cases involving discrimination, the key issue is often which tier of analysis should apply. Since the federal courts have clearly decided to evaluate military sexual orientation cases under the lower-tier "rational basis" test, the military's prospects of winning its case in court is greatly improved. In fact, on 6-9 January 1993, I attended the annual meeting of the Association of American Law Schools (AALS) in San Francisco at which the AALS Committee on Gay and Lesbian Legal Issues conducted a workshop entitled "Excluding Lesbians and Gay Men from Military Service: Whither the Policy, Whither the AALS." One of the speakers at this workshop, LAMBDA Legal Defense and Education Fund (a homosexual legal rights organization) attorney Mary Newcombe, frankly acknowledged that their constitutional case against the military exclusion policy is, in her words, "dead in the water" now that the courts have firmly decided upon the rational basis test.[10]

Another speaker at the workshop, Kate Dyer, editor of *Gays in Uniform* and former legislative assistant to Congressman Gerry Studds (D-Mass), was equally frank in acknowledging that they have no hope of persuading Congress to amend Article 125 (the sodomy provision) of the Uniform Code of Military Justice.[11] If homosexuals are admitted into the armed forces, therefore, they would enter with the certain knowledge that the very acts which define their life-style and come naturally to persons of their orientation, are illegal under the UCMJ.

On 29 January 1993, in a well-timed decision which accompanied President Clinton's announced intention to lift the gay ban, a Carter-appointed federal district court judge ruled in *Meinhold v. Department of Defense* (1993) that the Constitution forbids discharging Navy personnel solely because of homosexual orientation. However, the case involves a unique factual situation in which Meinhold served for twelve years, during which time he repeatedly acknowledged his homosexual orientation before senior officers and others. The Navy could have discharged him at any time, but for some reason no one took action to discharge him until 1992 when he proclaimed his homosexual orientation on an ABC television news program. As in Watkins, the court held that Meinhold was justified in relying upon the Navy's failure to discharge him in planning his future and assuming he could complete his Navy career.[12]

This factual situation, coupled with the Navy's apparent procedural errors and failure to fully articulate its rational basis, makes *Meinhold* an atypical case. Further, *Meinhold* is only a federal district court case and unlikely to set a precedent which the circuit courts of appeals or the Supreme Court will follow.

Because of these federal court precedents, the Supreme Court's ruling upholding state anti-sodomy laws in _Bowers v. Hardwick_, and the Court's many rulings upholding the authority of the armed forces to enforce good order and discipline, I am convinced that the present Supreme Court would uphold the military policy on homosexuality as constitutionally valid, probably by a vote of 7-2.

It is, of course, possible that President Clinton may appoint more liberal justices to the Court, and these justices may vote to strike down the policy. But it seems unlikely that President Clinton will alter the Court enough to change the outcome on a case of this nature during these next four years. Two of the justices most likely to leave office in the near future are the Court's most liberal justices, Blackmun and Stevens. Replacing them with new liberal justices would not alter the basic ideological make-up of the Court.

As stated in the beginning of this chapter, it is fashionable to compare the struggle of homosexuals for acceptance and legal rights with that of blacks in the 1950s and 1960s and that of women in the 1970s. But General Colin L. Powell, the first black ever to serve as chairman of the Joint Chiefs of Staff, rejects that comparison:

> I think the issues are quite different. Forty-odd years ago we already had blacks openly in the military and had had them for 100 years. It was a question of equal opportunity once they were in the military. And we were talking about something that was a fairly benign characteristic, with respect to skin color.
>
> With respect to gays in the military, it is, for us, a far more complicated issue that goes to one of the most fundamental of all human behavioral traits— sexual identity, sexual orientation, sexual preference.[13]

Focus on the more radical elements of the homosexual community and the analogy is faulty in other ways. As Horowitz observes,

> The civil rights movement, under the leadership of Martin Luther King, was guided by a conservative agenda. Its goal was to include black Americans in the existing social contract. . . .[14]

By contrast, Horowitz says, the goal of the homosexual revolutionaries is to destroy the existing social contract:

> It is this very principle of tolerance that [homosexual] revolutionaries and radicals most reject. For it is this rejection that defines them as radicals. For them, tolerance itself is repressive because it denies their most cherished illusion: that they are the authentic voice of humanity, and theirs the universal political solution.[15]

But, it is argued, the military ban on homosexuality applies not just to homosexual acts but to homosexual orientation as well. This orientation, some will say, is as much beyond a person's control as is the color of his skin.

Is homosexuality a condition, or a choice? While much research has been done on the subject, the causes of homosexuality are still unknown. Upbringing is often cited as a factor; children (especially boys) raised by a domineering or abusive father may develop an aversion to men in general; on the other hand, children of a passive father and a strong-willed mother may identify in character and role with the mother and women in general. Early contact or experience with pedophiles may also be a cause or contributing factor.

Other theorists cite genetics as the cause. In 1991 Dr. Simon LeVay reported his examination of the brains of thirty-five male cadavers, nineteen homosexual and sixteen heterosexual. The examination revealed that the cluster of neurons known as INAH3 was more than twice as large in heterosexual males as in homosexual males.[16] The implication is that homosexuality is the result of a brain condition that is beyond the person's control.

Dr. LeVay's study has been greeted with skepticism. First, the number of cadavers examined—thirty-five—is too small to provide definitive conclusions. Second, Dr. LeVay apparently failed to verify the sexual orientation of the sixteen supposedly heterosexual cadavers. Third, much variation existed among the cadavers of both orientations providing numerous other avenues along which common factors could be noted with differing results. And fourth, behavior can alter brain patterns. If the neuron clusters are related to sexual orientation at all, some argue, it is just as possible that homosexual behavior caused the smaller neuron clusters as that the smaller neuron clusters caused the homosexual behavior.[17]

There is some evidence that homosexuals can convert to heterosexuality, and this indicates that homosexuality is to some extent a matter of choice. In fact, about a third of males who report homosexual experience have engaged in homosexual behavior once or twice, and then never again.[18] Psychotherapy reports about a 30 percent cure rate, and others are prompted by religious or spiritual conversions.[19] Masters and Johnson report that many homosexuals convert or revert to heterosexuality, and that the prospects of doing so are good if one is motivated to change.[20] One reason more do not change may be that many mental health professionals do not regard homosexuality as abnormal and therefore do not encourage patients to change.

Whether homosexuality is a choice or a condition, the ultimate issue remains: Would lifting the military ban prejudice the good order and discipline of the armed forces and hinder the armed forces in accomplishing their mission? The main purpose of the military ban is not to "punish" homosexuals but to further the military mission of winning the nation's wars and deterring aggression. As noted earlier, military policy also excludes amputees, quadriplegics, persons with heart conditions, blind and deaf persons, those suffering from mental illness or retardation, and those of many other categories. No one seriously suggests that the military is "punishing" quadriplegics by excluding them from military service. Distinctions based on status are common in the armed forces and elsewhere.

Let us now consider the second argument:

(2) *The ban is unenforceable since homosexuals serve in the armed forces "under cover" anyway.*

There is no question that some homosexuals do serve in the armed forces despite the ban, and there is no question that some of them do engage in homosexual activity. The unanswered questions are, how many, and how much?

The fact that homosexuality persists does not mean the ban is unenforceable or should be repealed. The same reasoning could be applied to other problems: Murder is against the law, but people still commit murder; therefore, the ban on murder is unenforceable and should be repealed. Theft is against the law, but people still commit theft; therefore, the ban on theft is unenforceable and stealing should be made legal. Child abuse is against the law, but people still abuse children; therefore, the ban against child abuse is unenforceable and should be repealed. None of these parallels should shock us—in a more serious vein, the same argument is made for and seriously considered regarding the legalization of drugs.

Obviously, our criminal laws have not eliminated all murders, thefts, or abuse of children or drugs. That does not mean these laws are failures. The real question is, how much more murder, theft, child abuse, and drug abuse would take place if these practices were legalized? Likewise, the question is, how many more homosexuals would enter the military, and how many more homosexual acts would be performed, if the ban were eliminated?

Abigail Van Buren, in her famous "Dear Abby" column, recently wrote,

> Because so many gays are still in the closet, there are no reliable statistics on how many gays are serving honorably in the military, but a fairly good estimate would be 10 percent.[21]

But Ms. Van Buren's "fairly good estimate" (1) assumes the accuracy of the oft-cited Kinsey statistic for the general population, (2) assumes that the percentage of homosexuals in the military is the same as that of the general population, and (3) assumes that all of these are "serving honorably." So many assumptions threaten the accuracy of her estimate.

The fact is, no one knows how many homosexuals are serving in the armed forces. No one knows how many homosexuals ignore the ban and enlist anyway, or how many avoid military service in the first place because they perceive the military as an unfriendly environment for homosexuals, thereby pulling the percentage of homosexuals in the military below that of the general population, which as noted in chapter 1, is more appropriately estimated at about 2 percent.

Likewise, no one knows the extent to which homosexual acts are committed in the military. What do homosexuals do after they enlist? Do they continue the same practices with the same frequency as in civilian life, albeit a little more secretively? Or do they enlist, conceal their orientation, and refrain from homosexual activity? Do they abstain from sex entirely, or do they attempt heterosexual liaisons? Do some genuinely attempt to convert to heterosexuality? Do some try to abstain from homosexuality but occasionally find themselves overcome by desire? Do some continue homosexual activity, but with less frequency than in civilian life? Without answers to these questions, we are unable to say whether the ban has worked or not.

Furthermore, the fact that a law or policy has not been enforced does not mean it is unenforceable. The extent to which the ban has been enforced has varied from one service to another, as well as with the various commands, installations, and individual commanders. Many commanders who support the ban have chosen to enforce it only when homosexuality is brought to their attention; in most instances they have not actively sought out evidence of homosexual activity. And whichever course they follow, commanders are subject to criticism: If they vigorously enforce the ban, they are accused of "witch-hunting"; if they don't, they are accused of "hypocrisy" or "selectivity."

Justice White noted in *Bowers v. Hardwick* that law "is constantly based on notions of morality. . . ."[22] Morality and legality are not the same, but they cannot be entirely separated. Regardless of whether homosexuality is legalized, most military personnel will continue to regard homosexuality as immoral and/or distasteful and will refrain from homosexual behavior. A few will continue to engage in homosexual acts regardless of whether such acts are legal. In between, I believe, are many servicemen and women whose convictions, orientations, and identities are not clearly formed, in whose minds legality and morality are somewhat merged, and who are likely to think, "Well, if Uncle Sam says it's okay to engage in homosexuality, then why not try it?" This possibility is enhanced by the fact that a large portion of the force is composed of young people in their late teens or early twenties, an age group not known for their resoluteness when confronted with conflicting or opposing arguments.

In my opinion, the ban on homosexuality does deter many homosexuals from entering the armed forces. The number of homosexuals in the armed forces would rise substantially if the ban were lifted.

I further believe that the ban deters homosexuals who are in the armed forces from engaging in homosexual activity. While the ban does not completely stop them from engaging in homosexual activity, the deterrent effect of the ban does reduce the incidence of homosexual activity considerably. And, perhaps most importantly, the ban deters many who might be partially homosexual or uncertain about their sexual orientation or identity from experimenting with homosexual activity. One reason is that, with the ban in effect, such persons are less likely to be solicited by committed homosexuals.

And if, in a particular instance of a soldier whose duty performance is exemplary and whose private homosexual tendencies have not interfered with his work, his commander decides to close his eyes to the soldier's homosexuality and take no action, this flexible enforcement does not render the basic policy unworkable.

Let us now look at the third argument for lifting the ban:

(3) *The ban deprives the armed forces of a valuable manpower resource.*

If homosexuals constitute 10 percent of the general population, and if the ban prevents all of these people from entering the armed forces, then the armed forces have been effectively deprived of substantial manpower. But the argument is fallacious for several reasons.

First, the 10 percent figure is based upon Kinsey's misguided research. As noted earlier, there is good reason to believe Kinsey used faulty research methods which inflated his figures, and a figure of 2 percent is more realistic and more in line with other studies.

Second, the argument assumes that all of these people are excluded. To the extent that the second argument (that the ban is unenforceable) is valid, this third argument loses validity. For if homosexuals are already serving in the armed forces and the only question is whether they will serve legally or illegally, then the armed forces are not losing any manpower resources at all.

As noted above, however, I believe the ban does deter some homosexuals from entering the armed forces; so the armed forces do lose some manpower because of the ban. On the other hand, the number of homosexuals the military loses as a result of the ban, might be offset by the number of heterosexuals who might decide against military service if the ban were lifted. Many might object to sleeping, showering, and serving in the trenches with homosexuals, regardless of whether there is a valid basis for their objections. Many might perceive the armed forces as an immoral institution. Many parents who hold traditional values might be reluctant to recommend military service to their sons and daughters—and while one is legally an adult at age eighteen, the fact is that many young people continue to depend upon their parents for advice and counsel long after that age. As of this writing, in the few weeks that followed President Clinton's 29 January order that recruiters not ask enlistees about their sexual preferences, parents and recruiters have told me about several outstanding young recruits who have decided not to enlist because they don't want to serve with homosexuals.

The argument also assumes that those homosexuals who are serving, or who would serve if the ban were lifted, are or would be good performers. Some would be. There is no doubt that many homosexuals have been outstanding soldiers in every respect except for their sexual orientation. But is this true of all homosexuals? Or most? Or a disproportionate number? Or do a disproportionate number of homosexuals cause problems for the armed forces?

Lt. Col. Vickie S. Longenecker argues that

> Regardless of whether homosexuals constitute 3%, 10%, or 25% of the military, the fact remains that despite the DOD ban, homosexuals still enter and serve in the military in large numbers. In the majority of cases, they are performing as well as, if not better, than their heterosexual counterparts. According to DOD figures, of the 928 soldiers discharged for homosexuality during FY 90, only 80 received "other than honorable" discharges. The character of service of the overwhelming majority who were discharged (742, or 79.9%) was "honorable" as rated by their commanders (88 were not characterized). On the other hand, during the same time frame, of the 42,394 soldiers who were discharged for various reasons—ranging from unsatisfactory performance, disciplinary infractions, serious criminal offenses, etc.—only 22,706, or 53.5%, received discharges in the "honorable category." These facts alone would indicate that the overwhelming majority of homosexuals in the military were not dis-

charged because they could not do their job or because they adversely affected morale. Rather, they were discharged solely because of their "discovered" sexual preference or practice."[23]

Lt. Col. Longenecker's figures do not add up. To begin with, eighty "other than honorable" plus 742 "honorable" plus 88 "not characterized" equals 910, not 928. But the basic fallacy in Lt. Col. Longenecker's logic lies in her implicit assumption that all of those discharged for other causes were heterosexual. In fact, their sexual orientation is not known. Those who are discharged administratively under AFR 36-2 (officers) or 39-20 (enlisted) or comparable regulations in other services, are discharged for a wide variety of reasons: poor job performance, character and behavior disorders, financial irresponsibility, conflicts with authority, disrespect toward superiors, pattern of misconduct, criminal conviction in civilian court, etc. Some of these may be homosexual; some may be heterosexual. Those who are discharged for homosexuality are generally those who have had no other problems in the service. A soldier (homosexual or heterosexual) who has gone AWOL (absent without leave), abused drugs, or engaged in other misconduct will probably be discharged under one of those categories of AFR 39-10, and his sexual orientation will never be known. The fact that nearly 80 percent of those who were discharged for homosexuality received honorable discharges in 1990 indicates only that military authorities in that year were less harsh in their treatment of such persons than they were a decade or so earlier.

A more appropriate way to evaluate whether homosexuals perform well in the military would be to identify a large and representative sample of those who are discharged under AFR 39-10 or 36-2, ascertain their sexual orientation, and then calculate whether, in proportion to their total number in the force (which would also have to be determined), they were more or less likely than heterosexuals to be discharged for poor duty performance, conflicts with authority, financial irresponsibility, criminal convictions in civil court, or other grounds listed in AFR 39-10 and 36-2.

Another effective way to evaluate the performance of homosexuals in the military would be to identify a large and representative sample of homosexuals and heterosexuals and compare their Airman Performance Reports (APRs) and Officer Performance Reports (OPRs).

Williams and Weinberg cite several studies indicating that about 76 or 77 percent of homosexuals who serve in the armed forces receive honorable discharges.[24] In some instances they were discharged as homosexuals with honorable discharges, but in most instances they served their tours of duty and were discharged honorably with their sexual orientation never discovered. This demonstrates that it is possible for homosexuals to serve honorably. But about 98 percent of military personnel as a whole complete their enlistments and receive honorable discharges[25], so these figures actually indicate that the percentage of homosexuals who have problems in the military is several times higher than average.

Another fact to be considered is that, according to the GAO study, 24 percent of those discharged for homosexuality were in a non-occupational category (which includes patients, prisoners, and students) while only 9 percent of the military as a whole are in non-occupational categories.[26] There could be many explanations for this phenomenon, but it might indicate that homosexuals are more likely to be in nonproductive categories.

While it is true that many homosexuals have served with honor and some have even been decorated for valor, the same could be said for alcoholics, drug addicts, and pedophiles. This does not mean such persons belong in the armed forces.

Closely related to the manpower issue is the cost of replacing homosexuals who are discharged. The General Accounting Office noted that the cost of recruiting and providing initial training for an enlisted person is estimated to be $28,226, while the cost for an officer is $120,772. The GAO therefore concluded that each time a homosexual is removed from the service, the armed forces incur at least this cost in replacing that person, not counting the cost of the investigation and discharge proceedings themselves.[27]

The Department of Defense, in its response to the GAO study, commented:

> Nonconcur. Each year the Department of Defense separates about 300,000 Service members, approximately 100,000 of whom are separated for force management reasons. Homosexuals make up less than one-third of 1 percent of that total.
>
> In estimating the cost, the GAO apparently assumed that none of those separated for homosexuality would be lost through normal attrition or for force management reasons. There also was no recognition that approximately one-half the enlisted force does not serve beyond the initial enlistment. The GAO cost estimate is, therefore, well in excess of what reasonably could be projected under normal circumstances.[28]

Furthermore, since the total force is currently being reduced in number, if homosexuals were not discharged, others would be discharged in their place. The cost of discharging them, therefore, appears to be reduced to zero.

Undoubtedly, the armed forces will lose some good performers if the ban is retained. In some instances the cost of replacing these people may be substantial, though not as high as GAO estimated. However, these costs might be more than offset by the other increased costs that could result from legalizing homosexuality. One of these might be increased cost of health care through an AIDS epidemic and other diseases, as the next chapter will demonstrate.

One related manpower factor is the possibility that the performance of homosexuals in the military would improve if the ban were lifted, because they would no longer be under the stress that results from their legal predicament and the secrecy it requires. However, if homosexuals cannot function under this kind of stress, how can they be expected to handle the stress of combat? Certainly, homosexuals in the military do experience considerable stress because of their orientation and its stigma. However, legalizing homosexuality would not entirely remove that stigma. And to whatever extent it would remove the stigma, the effect its removal would have upon duty performance is purely speculative.

Finally, opponents of the gay ban resort to coercion: The armed forces will lose manpower, they maintain, because some universities will not allow them to recruit on campus so long as they discriminate against homosexuals. At present there are no statistics as to how many, if any, universities impose such a prohibition, and what effect such a prohibition has on military recruitment. It is just as possible that other schools, notably religious or church-affiliated schools, might bar military recruiters if the armed forces hired homosexuals. In any event, military policy should be determined according to the good order and discipline of the armed forces, and military leaders should not allow themselves to be intimidated by those who would, in effect, try to deny their students the right to receive information about a military career.

Nonetheless, if gay rights advocates do resort to such intimidation and coercion, military recruiters have a weapon of their own—a little-known Department of Defense regulation (32 CFR Sec. 216) which authorizes the DOD to cut off DOD funds to universities or university programs that refuse to allow military recruiters. There is no reason this regulation could not be used, if necessary, to protect the right of military recruiters to give, and the right of students to receive, information about a military career. It is ironic that some of those who speak so loudly about nondiscrimination and freedom of expression, will themselves be the first to discriminate and deny that freedom to others when they may advance their own interests by doing so.

The words of David Horowitz are worth repeating, even though he is speaking about the radical fringe of the gay rights movement that may not represent homosexuals as a whole:

> It is this very principle of tolerance that [homosexual] revolutionaries and radicals most reject. For it is this rejection that defines them as radicals. For them, tolerance itself is repressive because it denies their most cherished illusion: that they are the authentic voice of humanity, and theirs the universal political solution.[29]

Arguments against lifting the ban on homosexuals run the gamut from moral and theological to personal, hygienic, constitutional, legal, disciplinary, and practical. Some arguments are persuasive to some; others are more persuasive to others. Let us examine each in turn.

Issue #1:
Against Admitting Homosexuals
into the Armed Forces:
The Moral Issue

The moral values of Western civilization are derived largely from the Judeo-Christian tradition, which in turn is derived largely from the Bible. Those who explored, settled, and founded this nation held to that tradition. Even those few who probably were not orthodox Christians, like Jefferson and Franklin, were raised in the church and based their values upon Judeo-Christian morality.[1]

It is not surprising, therefore, that American society has traditionally regarded homosexuality with strong disapproval, for the Bible, both Old and New Testaments, strongly condemns homosexuality. A brief survey of the relevant Bible passages makes this very clear:

- *Genesis 1:27* So God created man in his own image, in the image of God created he him; male and female created he them.

- *Genesis: 9:19-29* narrates a drunken homosexual encounter between Noah and his son, Ham, and God's strong condemnation of this act.

61

- *Genesis 9:19-29 (cf II Peter 2:6-10, Jude 7)* describes God's destruction of the cities of Sodom and Gomorrah because of their sexual practices. From Sodom we derive the word "sodomy." While gay rights advocates have tried to interpret this passage as applying only to homosexual rape, nothing in the passage would justify that limitation. In fact, if that were true, it would seem that God would have destroyed only the homosexual rapists and not their innocent victims.

- *Leviticus 18:22-29* Thou shalt not lie with mankind, as with womankind; it is abomination. Neither shalt thou lie with any beast to defile thyself therewith: neither shall any woman stand before a beast to lie down thereto; it is confusion. Defile not yourselves in any of these things: for in all these the nations are defiled which I cast out before you: and the land is defiled: therefore I do visit the iniquity thereof upon it, and the land itself vomiteth out her inhabitants. Ye shall therefore keep my statutes and my judgment, and shall not commit any of these abominations; neither any of your own nation, nor any stranger that sojourneth among you: (for all these abominations have the men of the land done, which was before you, and the land is defiled;) that the land spew not you out also, when ye defile it, as it spewed out the nations that were before you. For whosoever shall commit any of these abominations, even the souls that commit them shall be cut off from among their people. [NOTE: The Canaanites, whom the Israelites displaced at God's command according to Scripture, regularly practiced homosexuality, prostitution involving both sexes as part of their religious fertility rights, sex with idols with artificial phalluses, child sacrifice as part of sexual orgies, and other such practices.]

• *Deuteronomy 23:17* There shall be no whore of the daughters of Israel, nor a sodomite of the sons of Israel.

• *Romans 1:26-27* For this cause [man's rebellion against God] God also gave them up unto vile affections: for even their women did change the natural use into that which is against nature: and likewise also the men, leaving the natural use of the woman, burned in their lust one toward another; men with men working that which is unseemly, and receiving in themselves that recompense of their error which was meet. [NOTE: The phrase "burned in their lust toward one another" implies a condemnation of homosexual tendencies as well as homosexual acts.]

• *I Corinthians 6:9-10* Know ye not that the unrighteous shall not inherit the kingdom of God? Be not deceived; neither fornicators, nor idolators, nor adulterers, nor effeminate, nor abusers of themselves with mankind, nor thieves, nor covetous, nor drunkards, nor revilers, nor extortioners shall inherit the kingdom of God.

• *I Timothy 1:9-10* Knowing this, that the law is not made for a righteous man, but for the lawless and disobedient, for the ungodly and sinners, for unholy and profane, for murderers of fathers and murders of mothers, for manslayers, for whoremongers, for them that defile themselves with mankind, for menstealers, for liars, for perjured persons, and if there be any other thing that is contrary to sound doctrine. . . .

Gay rights advocates dismiss religious objections as overly narrow interpretations of Scripture. But it is clear from the above passages that one need not interpret them too "narrowly" to reach the general conclusion that the Bible disapproves of homosexuality.

Others suggest that the condemnation is cultural; the Bible passages quoted above mean homosexuality was frowned upon in those times but those prohibitions do not necessarily apply today. But these passages condemn homosexuality in the same context as many other sins, such as murder, which obviously apply to all cultures. Furthermore, the Genesis events took place thousands of years, and were recorded at least 1,400 years, before the New Testament epistles.

Closely related is the argument that these passages apply only to that time because then it was necessary to "be fruitful and multiply" (Genesis 1:22) and "replenish the earth" (Genesis 9:1). But the language is nowhere limited to that time period; in fact, the Genesis 9 passage occurs in the context of the covenant God made with Noah which applies to all time, all people, and all generations (9:9, 10, 12, 16). Also, the Mosaic Law was recorded centuries after God made his covenant with Noah, and the New Testament epistles were written at least 1,400 years after Moses recorded the Law. Clearly these prohibitions spanned a period of thousands of years. It could be argued just as convincingly that the command against murder was contextual and no longer applies since replenishing the earth is no longer a pressing need, and human life is, therefore, now expendable.

The suggestion of gay rights advocates that David and Jonathan (I Samuel 18:1-4; 20:16-18) were homosexual lovers is utterly without foundation and misunderstands the Hebrew word for love (*ahabah*) which is

used in a pure sense and frequently denotes God's love
for man; the kiss (I Samuel 20:41) was a standard form
of friendly greeting in Hebrew culture as well as other
cultures and in no way implies homosexuality. Likewise
the suggestion that Jesus and the Apostle John were
homosexuals because John is called the apostle whom
Jesus loved (John 13:23; 20:2), is not only without foundation but reflects a misunderstanding of the Greek
words for love (*agape* and *phileo*, as against *eros*). The
fact that gay rights advocates feel compelled to use such
far-fetched examples to justify their actions by Scripture
demonstrates how weak their case really is.

Lt. Col. Vickie S. Longenecker calls the Church's
position on homosexuality "intolerant" and says,

> Because of the limited knowledge in human sexu-
> ality of the time, Biblical writers believed there was
> only one form of sexuality, namely heterosexuality.
> Therefore, heterosexuals participating in
> homosexualism were sinners because they had gone
> against their nature as heterosexuals. Likewise, in
> several New Testament passages, St. Paul condemns
> any behavior that exchanges the natural for the
> unnatural and raises the question of authentic
> personhood. Paul suggests that the real "sin" is in
> not being true to one's nature (i.e., a heterosexual
> participating in homosexualism, or a homosexual
> participating in heterosexualism).[2]

Lt. Col. Longenecker's interpretation of Paul is, at
best, highly imaginative. First, her interpretation of Paul
is inconsistent with the Old Testament passages. Second, the basic message of all of Paul's writings is not
that one should be true to one's nature, but precisely
the opposite. Paul's gospel is that man is by nature sinful
and unclean (Romans 2:14; 7:17-18; 7:23-25; 8:1-8;
Ephesians 2:3), that unfortunately he does follow his

nature (Romans 7:15-25), and that he needs the grace of God to change (Ephesians 2:8-16; Galatians 5:17-24). Rather than being "true to one's nature," one should "be transformed by the renewing of your mind, that ye may prove what is that good, and acceptable, and perfect, will of God" (Romans 12:2).

Far from having only "limited knowledge in human sexuality," the biblical writers were very familiar with the homosexual practices of Sodom, Gomorrah, Canaan, and other pagan cultures. And Lt. Col. Longenecker ignores the possibility that the writers of Scripture may have been inspired by a higher and wiser Source (i.e., God) as Jews and Christians have traditionally believed.

In societies that are based upon Judaism and Christianity, and Islam as well, homosexuality has been strongly disapproved. Nor has this disapproval been limited to societies dominated by these three religions. Even before Christianity took hold in England, the early Ynglings or Anglo-Saxons had a system of justice in which most offenses were considered crimes against an individual victim rather than against society as a whole. Only four offenses were considered crimes against society—treason, cowardice in battle, desertion, and homosexuality—and all four were punishable by death.[3] Note that three of the four are undeniably military-related offenses and the fourth has a case being made for itself in this book.

While it is true that some primitive societies did tolerate or encourage homosexuality, such as the Swanis of Africa[4], or the various reprobate cultures described in the Bible, most did not. In fact, in most primitive societies, homosexuality was strongly condemned.

Gay rights advocates frequently cite Greece as an example of the flowering of homosexuality. Apparently homosexuality was widespread among the ancient Greeks, but it was by no means universal. In fact, in Athens those who received homosexual attentions were officially disenfranchised, though the practice was widely tolerated. It appears that homosexuality became more widespread as Greece degenerated in other ways, as is true of other societies.[5]

During most of Rome's history, homosexuality was illegal. In fact, homosexuality was a capital crime under the Theodosian Code (Theodosian Code 9.7.6) and under the Justinian Code (Justinian Code 9.9.31). Nevertheless it existed, introduced in part through Rome's conquest of Greece.[6] Julius Caesar apparently was bisexual. (So was Nero, but gay rights advocates are much less likely to point that out.)[7] But homosexuality seemed to flower during Rome's periods of decadence and fade during periods of rebuilding and revival under emperors such as Domitian[8] and Marcus Aurelius.[9] And even while homosexuality flourished, Romans seemed to recognize it as perversion. The historian Livy describes it as "defilement,"[10] and Cicero referred to a group of rebel soldiers as "perfumed perverts."[11] Besides homosexuality, Greeks and Romans tolerated slavery, practiced pedophilia, exposed unwanted infants to death by negligence and abandonment, and treated women and children as property—hardly a model that Americans would want to emulate.

In fact, throughout world history, homosexuality generally has been regarded as an aberration. Certainly there have been homosexuals who have excelled in various fields of endeavor, including military service. The fact that gay rights leaders have to strain so hard to find successful military leaders who were homosexual or bisexual, jumping from Alexander to Caesar to Lawrence of Arabia, demonstrates that these are the exception rather than the rule.

The condemnation of homosexuality has not been limited to Judeo-Christian societies. Muslims and others have likewise disapproved of homosexuality. (I fear the fate of a homosexual U.S. soldier in the Middle East who is caught in the act by the Saudis!) Throughout history there has been a general recognition that heterosexuality is in accord with nature while homosexuality is contrary to nature, whether "nature" is perceived as a divine order or simply the natural state.

While it is sometimes said that morality should not be confused with legality, the two cannot be entirely separated. As the Supreme Court noted in *Bowers v. Hardwick* (1986), the law "is constantly based on notions of morality, and if all laws representing essentially moral choices are to be invalidated under the Due Process Clause, the courts will be very busy indeed."[12] As Chief Justice Burger wrote, speaking for the majority in *Paris Adult Theatre v. Slaton* (1973), a case involving obscene films in commercial theaters:

> . . . [T]here are legitimate state interests at stake in stemming the tide of commercialized obscenity. . . . These include the interest of the public itself in the quality of life and the total community environment, the tone of commerce in the great city centers, and, possible, the public safety itself.
>
> . . . In deciding Roth, this Court implicitly accepted that a legislature could legitimately act on such a conclusion to protect "the social interest in order and morality." Roth v. U.S., supra, 354 U.S. at 485. . . .[13]

In his famous lecture series *The Enforcement of Morals*, the British Lord Justice Patrick Devlin declared "the suppression of vice is as much the law's business as the suppression of subversive activities," because "what makes a society is a community of ideas, not political ideas alone, but also ideas about the way its members should behave and govern their lives." For this reason, Lord Devlin said, government may restrain and punish conduct which meets with widespread "intolerance, indignation and disgust."[14]

The fact that moral objections to homosexuality are based in part upon religious convictions does not make the ban on homosexuality unconstitutional. As the Supreme Court has recognized in *Harris v. McRae* (1980), the mere fact that a statute happens to be consistent with the tenets of one or more religions does not, without more, render the statute unconstitutional.[15] And in *Church of the Holy Trinity v. United States* (1982), the Supreme Court cited a long history of earlier cases concluding that "the Christian religion is part of the common law of Pennsylvania,"[16] and, by implication, of the United States—apparently speaking of Christianity not in terms of specific doctrines of Christianity but in terms of the moral values Christianity teaches.

Using similar reasoning in *Late Corporation of the Church of Jesus Christ of Latter Day Saints v. United States* (1890) the Supreme Court upheld as constitutional a ban on polygamy in the territory of Utah, ruling that polygamy "is contrary to the spirit of Christianity and of the civilization which Christianity has produced in the Western world."[17] In a similar case the Court ruled that "Bigamy and polygamy are crimes by the laws of all civilized and Christian countries. . . ."[18] While these cases are seldom cited today, they have never been overruled.

Likewise the Court has consistently held that federal and state governments have authority to suppress lotteries, simply because they constitute a moral "pestilence."[19] The Court's decision to uphold the Georgia anti-sodomy statute in _Bowers v. Hardwick_ is consistent with this reasoning and these precedents. If a state government has the authority to enforce moral judgments on issues such as homosexuality, the armed forces have much more authority to do so. Aside from issues concerning the good order and discipline of the military, we must remember that the armed forces consist largely of young, single men and women—and as noted before, while one becomes legally an adult at age eighteen, one does not achieve maturity overnight on one's eighteenth birthday. The vast majority of these young men and women are serving at duty assignments far from home, family, school, church, and the other influences which provide stability and restrain their behavior. In the absence of such restraining influences, the military needs to provide another means of maintaining high moral standards. Noting that "a large portion of those enlisting are under twenty-one years of age" and "are in a very formative period of their lives," General John A. Lejeune, the 13th Commandant of the Marine Corps, declared,

> We owe it to them, to their parents, and to the nation, that when discharged from the services they should be far better physically, mentally, and morally than they were when they enlisted.[20]

Furthermore, the armed forces are currently 90 percent male, and most of these are young, single men. If the ban on homosexuality were eliminated, one could easily see the military becoming a magnet for homosexuals. The image of the armed forces will suffer greatly if soldiers are perceived as largely homosexual or otherwise immoral or perverted. With this public perception, few will proudly wear the uniform.

It is much better for the armed forces to be perceived as the last bastion of encoded traditional morality, than as a cesspool of immorality and a haven for the promiscuous.

5

Issue #2:
The Health Issue

An effective fighting force must be physically healthy. In any discussion of the military ban on homosexuals, the subject of Acquired Immune Deficiency Syndrome (AIDS) cannot be ignored.

Gay rights advocates are often reluctant to address this subject. The AIDS epidemic arose right at the time homosexuals were pushing for public acceptance and legal recognition. Understandably, they feared the AIDS epidemic could cause a public backlash against homosexuality. In the detection, treatment, and prevention of AIDS, great care has been taken to protect the rights and privacy of AIDS victims. (AIDS has been described as the only disease with civil rights, and AIDS victims have been described as the first group of sick people with political savvy.)

This fact remains: According to the Centers for Disease Control, nearly two-thirds of all AIDS cases in the United States are directly attributable to homosexual activity.[1] If the much-quoted Kinsey figure is correct and homosexuals constitute 10 percent of the total population, then homosexuals are about eighteen times more likely to spread or acquire AIDS than are heterosexuals.

73

If, as I believe, Kinsey's figures are inflated and the percentage of homosexuals is actually closer to 2 percent, then homosexuals are 147 times more likely to acquire or spread AIDS.[2]

The health danger is not limited to AIDS. Robert Knight writes that

> a compilation of recent health studies shows that homosexuals account for a disproportionate number of America's most serious sexually transmitted diseases. Homosexual youths are 23 times more likely to contract a sexually-transmitted disease than heterosexual youths. Lesbians are 19 times more likely than heterosexual women to have had syphilis, twice as likely to suffer from genital warts, and four times as likely to have scabies. Male homosexuals are 14 times more likely to have had syphilis than male heterosexuals.[3]

Knight's conclusions are corroborated by other sources. In his study of ninety-three homosexuals, Dr. Gold found that 65.5 percent had had gonorrhea, 52.5 percent had had hepatitis, 49.5 percent had had ameobiasis, 40.8 percent had had venereal warts, 39.7 percent had had phthirus pubis, 36.7 percent had had syphilis, 26.8 percent had had nonspecific urethritis, 22.9 percent had had genital herpes simplex, 16.1 percent had had shigellosis, 10.7 percent had had giardiasis, 10.7 percent had had nonspecific proctitis, and 6.4 percent had had scabies.[4]

Drs. Ernst and Houts reached similar conclusions:

> In addition to high rates of gonorrhea, syphilis, and hepatitis B, gay men have been shown to be at high risk for venereal transmission of anorectal venereal warts, hepatitis A, enteric pathogens, and cytomegalovirus infection. The recently described acquired immune deficiency syndrome (AIDS) involving

opportunistic infections such as Pneumocystis carinii pneumonia and Kaposi's sarcoma accentuate the public and personal health risk associated with sexually promiscuous gay males.[5]

Likewise, Dr. Anne C. Collier, M.D., has noted that "A past history of sexually transmitted diseases was given by 160 (89 percent) of 180 homosexual men compared with 12 (46 percent) of the 26 heterosexual clinic patients."[6] Dr. Miriam J. Alter concluded that "Hepatitis B infection occurred at rates of 40% to 60% among homosexual men, compared with 4% to 18% among heterosexual men."[7]

The practices of homosexuals are the likely reason for this higher risk of disease. As noted earlier, homosexuals are likely to engage in sex with a much greater number of partners than are heterosexuals. For example, a Kinsey study concluded that the average practicing homosexual had more than 250 partners during his lifetime; 43 percent claimed to have had sex with 500 or more partners; and almost 30 percent reported having 1,000 or more partners.[8] Other studies reached similar figures. Having sex with such a large number of partners obviously puts one at increased risk of contracting or transmitting disease.

Homosexual practices increase the risk. We have previously seen, also, that homosexuals commonly engage in oral and anal sex; well over 90 percent engage in anal intercourse, and over 60 percent engage in analingual (tongue in anus) sex.[9] Homosexuals are much more likely to engage in such practices as sex with animals, urinating or defecating upon their partners, placing their fingers or even their fists or foreign objects in their partners' rectums, and sadomasochism.[10] In the course of these activities they are much more likely to come into contact with feces, urine, semen, blood, or saliva.

Condoms do not solve the problem. Whether it's due to apathy or heat of passion, large numbers do not use condoms even though they have been instructed to do so, and many who do use condoms, use them incorrectly. Even when used correctly, the condom has a high failure rate. According to the _British Medical Journal_, during homosexual activity condoms rupture about 11 percent of the time and slip off about 15 percent of the time.[11] Since the AIDS virus is smaller than the sperm cell and can pass through a condom more easily, the failure of the condom to effectively prevent AIDS and other diseases is not surprising.

Contact with feces is a particular problem, with anal or analingual sex. Homosexuals sometimes try to avoid this problem by using enemas or rectal douching, but this does not completely eliminate the problem, and it may in fact increase the risk of viral transmission through the rectum.[12] The problem is accentuated when fellatio follows anal sex.

Unlike the vagina, the tissue of the rectum is very thin, very fragile, and very easily lacerated. (It might be said that the rectum was not designed to be a sex organ.) Because of the technical nature of this material, it is best to let the medical experts speak for themselves. Writing in _Surgery, Gynecology and Obstetrics_, Dr. James E. Barone says,

> The incidence of trauma to the rectum, secondary to homosexual practices, is increasing . . . 112 patients with trauma of the rectum or with retained foreign bodies, or both, resulting from homosexual or autoerotic practices, were seen.[13]

Likewise Dr. Kingsley says in _Diseases of the Colon and Rectum_,

Anorectal injuries and retained colorectal foreign bodies secondary to homosexual activities, sexual assaults, and transanal autoeroticism are common occurrences in the present society.[14]

Dr. Irving B. Margolis wrote in *Surgery, Gynecology and Obstetrics* that

symptomatic anorectal disease is more common among homosexual men than among heterosexuals. In approximately two-thirds of the patients, careful study will reveal an etiologic agent for proctitis. The remainder will be classified as "gay bowel syndrome."[15] [NOTE: The term "gay bowel syndrome" was coined for infection of or trauma to the rectum or anus, because it occurs commonly as a result of homosexual activity.]

And Dr. Barone adds,

A series of 101 patients with trauma of the rectum, secondary to homosexual practices, presenting at this hospital is reviewed. Two patients were injured twice. Thirty-six patients had retained foreign bodies in the rectum, 55 had lacerations of the mucosa, two had disruptions of the anal sphincter and ten had perforations of the rectosigmoid.[16]

According to Dr. Gottesman in *Diseases of the Colon and Rectum,*

The accurate diagnosis of free perforation in rectal trauma is also important. In the homosexual community, fist fornication is becoming increasingly common.[17]

The result, Dr. Barone says, is serious injury to the rectum:

Serious injuries, secondary to homosexual acts, can and do occur, as evidenced by the mortality reported in this series. Perforations of the rectosigmoid above the peritoneal reflection can be treated by laparotomy, repair of the perforation, removal of gross [fecal] contamination by irrigation, proximal loop colostomy and appropriate antibiotic therapy. Perforations below the peritoneal reflection are challenging instances which require individualized management.[18]

A further chilling result, according to Dr. Holly, is cancer:

Anal cancer risk for men who expressed a homosexual preference [was] more than 12 times that for heterosexual men [with a 2.7 risk factor].[19]

Homosexuals appear to suffer extensively from emotional problems as well. Dr. J. Hampton Atkinson has observed that "it is generally true that more persons in the . . . homosexual groups [studied] . . . regardless of medical status, experienced depressive and anxiety disorders more than did heterosexual controls."[20] Dr. Chris Anne Raymond reports that suicide ideation occurred in more than 50 percent of the homosexuals she studied, and that 20 percent had attempted suicide at least once.[21] The special stress and demands of military life could accentuate these emotional problems, hinder discipline and morale, and thereby jeopardize the military mission.

Defenders of homosexuality insist that these emotional problems are caused by social disapproval and the need for secrecy. But Weinberg and Williams, two researchers sympathetic toward homosexual problems, compared the emotional problems of homosexuals in the United States with those of homosexuals in the Netherlands and Denmark (two of the countries most accepting of homosexuals) and found the problems were the same: "The distress does not decrease as tolerance is increased."[22]

Added to all of this, a report by the National Lesbian-Gay Health Foundation recently acknowledged that homosexuals are about three times as likely as heterosexuals to have alcohol or drug abuse problems.[23]

The result is that homosexuals have a relatively short average life expectancy of forty-one years—nor can this be attributed entirely to AIDS, for the average life expectance of AIDS victims is thirty-nine years. Only 1 percent of homosexuals die of old age; less than 3 percent are over age fifty-five.[24]

In the face of all of this evidence—AIDS, other disease, rectal injury, rectal cancer, emotional problems, alcohol and drug abuse, suicide, shortened life expectancy—one cannot help wondering why homosexuals would persist in a life-style that is in fact a "death-style." David Horowitz's graphic description of the homosexual revolutionary may not be speaking of the average homosexual, but his portrait of some of the leaders of the gay rights movement is chilling:

> In rejecting America's normative institutions, while radically inventing the social future, however, they invite just those retributions that have historically attended the systematic violation of natural order. In so doing, they have created their own social Frankenstein, even without achieving state power, in the contemporary epidemic of AIDS.
>
> Who would not have known in 1969, the year of "Gay Liberation," for example, that promiscuous anal sex was unsanitary for individuals and a potential danger to public health? Yet, gay liberation was defined by its theorists as just that: promiscuous anal sex, a challenge to the repressive "sex-negative" culture of what [homosexual] theorists now call "heteronormativity," i.e., the heterosexual and monogamous norm. In the radical view, existing social norms reflected nothing about humanity's

historic experience, but were merely a social construction to preserve the privileges of a dominant group.

. . . Gay liberation was identified with a sexual agenda that did not seek civic tolerance, respect, and integration of homosexuals into the public order of bourgeois life. It was defined instead as a defiant promiscuity, the overthrow of bourgeois morals and sexual restraints. And, consequently, of bourgeois standards of public hygiene. No natural or moral barriers were recognized to the realization of the radical project.

The effect of this radical agenda was immediate and unmistakable. In the years 1967-1969—the flowering of the sexual revolution—the incidence of amoebiasis, a parasitic sexually transmitted disease, increased _fifty_ times in San Francisco because of promiscuous oral-anal sex among gays. Despite the consequences, a Toronto leftist paper defended the practice in an article titled "Rimming [analingual or tongue-in-anus sex] As a Revolutionary Act." During the next decade, the tolerant American civil order made room for the sexual revolutionaries. Public officials licensed sexual gymnasia called "bathhouses" and turned a blind eye toward homosexual activity in bookstore back rooms, bars, and "glory hole" establishments, until a $100 million industry flourished by decade's end. At the same time, natural forces asserted themselves with ever more devastating result.

As opportunistic but still treatable infections flourished in the Petri dish of the liberated culture, gay radicals merely increased their defiance. Overloaded VD clinics became trusting places in the liberated culture. In his authoritative history of the AIDS epidemic, author Randy Shilts describes the atmosphere on the eve of its outbreak: "Gay men were being washed up by tide after tide of increasingly serious infections. First it was syphilis and gonorrhea. Gay men made up about 80% of the 70,000 annual patient visits to [San Francisco's] VD clinics. Easy treatment had imbued them with such a cavalier attitude toward venereal diseases that many gay men saved their waiting-line numbers, like little tokens of desirability, and the clinic was considered an easy place to pick up both a shot and a date."

Far from causing radical activists to rethink their agenda, the burgeoning epidemics prompted them to escalate their assault. When Dr. Dan William, a gay specialist, warned of the danger of continued promiscuity, he was publicly denounced as a "monogamist" in the gay press. When playwright Larry Kramer issued a similar warning, he was accused in the *New York Native* of "gay homophobia and antieroticism." At a public meeting in the year preceding the first AIDS cases, Edmund White, co-author of *The Joy of Gay Sex*, proposed that "gay men should wear their sexually transmitted diseases like red badges of courage in a war against a sex-negative society." Michael Callen, a gay youth present at the meeting, had already had 3,000 sexual partners and was shortly to come down with AIDS. He writes in his book, *Surviving AIDS*, that when he heard White's triumphant defiance of nature's law, he thought: "Every time I get the clap [gonorrhea] I'm striking a blow for the sexual revolution."

Callen's attitude was emblematic. The first clusters of AIDS were formed not by monogamous civil reformers who had come out of the closet to demand tolerance and respect, but by sexual revolutionaries who pushed their bodies' immune envelopes to advance the new order. Callen, who later founded People With AIDS, reflected on this revolutionary path: "Unfortunately, as a function of a microbiological . . . certainty, this level of sexual activity resulted in concurrent epidemics of syphilis, gonorrhea, hepatitis, amoebiasis, venereal warts and, we discovered too late, other pathogens. Unfortunately, and with the best of revolutionary intentions, a small subset of gay men managed to create disease settings equivalent to those of poor third-world nations in one of the richest nations on earth."

The diseases were being transformed as well. As Shilts explains, the enteric diseases—amoebiasis, Gay Bowel Syndrome, giardiasis, and shigellosis—were followed by an epidemic of hepatitis B, "a disease that had transformed itself, via the popularity of anal intercourse, from a blood-borne scourge into a venereal disease."

Where were public health officials, as these epidemics took their toll? Why didn't they intervene, sound the alarm, close the bathhouses, undertake vigorous education campaigns among gays to warn potential victims of the danger in their path? The reason was the revolution itself: So successful was the campaign of the radical activists that it made traditional public health practices politically impossible, particularly when officials attempted to close sexual bathhouses regarded as "symbols of gay liberation." As Don Francis, the Centers for Disease Control official in charge of fighting the hepatitis B epidemic, told a reporter: "We didn't intervene because we felt that it would be interfering with an alternative lifestyle."

In the early eighties, the AIDS epidemic was still confined to three cities with large homosexual communities. Aggressive public health methods might have prevented the epidemic's outward spread. But every effort to take normal precautionary measures was thwarted in turn by the political juggernaut the gay liberation movement had managed to create. Under intense pressure from gay activists, for example, the director of public health of the City of

San Francisco refused to close bathhouses, maintaining that they were valuable centers of "education" about AIDS, even though their only purpose was to facilitate promiscuous sex.

Not only were measures to prevent the geographical spread of AIDS thwarted by radical politics, but measures to prevent its spread into other communities were obstructed as well. Thus when officials tried to institute screening procedures for the nation's blood banks and asked the gay community not to make donations while the epidemic persisted, gay political leaders opposed the procedures as infringing the "right" of homosexuals to give blood. The San Francisco Coordinating Committee of Gay and Lesbian Services, chaired by Pat Norman, a city official, issued a policy paper asserting that donor screening was "reminiscent of miscegenation blood laws that divided black blood from white" and "similar in concept to the World War II rounding up of Japanese Americans in the western half of the country to minimize the possibility of espionage."

The result of these revolutionary attitudes was to spread AIDS among hemophiliacs and some heterosexuals. Similar campaigns against testing and contact tracing—standard procedures in campaigns against other sexually transmitted diseases—insured the metastasis of AIDS into the black and Hispanic communities, which now account for more than 50 percent of the known cases.

The war against civilization and nature, which is at the heart of the radical enterprise, inevitably produces monsters like AIDS. The epidemic has now taken a toll of 200,000 Americans, with a million more infected. The implementation of real public health methods is nowhere in sight. Thus, even as the ashes of the Communist empire grow cold, the lessons of the disaster have not been learned. Once in power—as the entire history of our bloody century attests—the radical impulse embraces radical evil in the futile attempt to enforce its rule, and to realize its impossible ideal. The nihilism that rejects nature and the idea of the normal is as blindly destructive as its consequences are predictable.[25]

The demand of radical gay activists that military recruits not be tested for HIV[26] might seem suicidal, but it is consistent with radical gay theory which, as Horowitz says, rebels against even "bourgeois standards of public hygiene." While these advocates of homosexual revolution do not necessarily speak for all or even most homosexuals, they indeed command public attention.

The health risks associated with homosexuality deserve central consideration in any serious discussion of military policy toward homosexuality, for the health (physical and mental) of service members is essential if the military is to be an effective fighting force. The evidence clearly demonstrates that homosexuals are highly prone to many diseases. Since many who engage in homosexual activity are actually bisexual, there is a strong likelihood that they could spread these diseases to heterosexuals as well. In combat situations the close physical contact, the presence of blood, the need for on-the-spot blood transfusions further increase the risk. The conclusion that the entry of homosexuals into the armed forces will lead to major health problems for the entire force is inescapable.

The Jewish War Veterans of the United States have calculated that each AIDS case costs the military approximately $200,000 and that the armed forces have spent $3,000,000,000 on AIDS-related medical costs over the past ten years.[27] Dr. Ann Hardy, et al, in 1986 calculated that about $147,000 was at that time being spent for hospital care for each AIDS patient—and this does not include out-of-hospital care.[28] If that was true in January 1986, the Jewish War Veterans' estimate of $200,000 for 1992 is realistic or even conservative. Using a Consumer Price Index rise of 6.5 percent per year, Major R.D. Adair and Captain Joseph C. Myers estimate that the cost will grow to about $386,000 per patient by the year 2000, and nearly $639,000 per patient by the year 2008.[29] The cost of a major AIDS epidemic in the armed forces is incalculable, considering that the taxpayers pay the cost of most health care for military personnel and their families.

The spread of disease, medical costs, time lost from work, premature deaths are a serious cost that cannot be measured solely in economic terms. The effect on morale and welfare must also be considered, not to mention the overall human tragedy involved.

include out-of-hospital care." If that was true in January 1986, the Jewish War Veterans' estimate of $200,000 for 1992 is realistic or even conservative. Using a Consumer Price Index rise of 6.9 percent per year, Major R.D. Adair and Captain Joseph C. Myers estimate that the cost will grow to about $580,000 per patient by the year 2000, and nearly $939,000 per patient by the year 2008. The gravity of this AIDS epidemic in the armed forces is unmistakable, considering that the taxpayers pay the cost of most health care for military personnel and their families.

The spread of disease, medical costs, time lost from work, premature deaths are a serious cost that cannot be measured solely in economic terms. The effect on morale and welfare must also be considered, not to mention the overall human tragedy involved.

Issue #3:
Pedophilia and Other Crimes

Approximately one-third of all child molestations involve homosexual activity.[1]

That means the remaining two-thirds are committed by heterosexuals. But in assessing the risk, we must consider the proportion of homosexuals to the total population. Suppose we accept the oft-quoted figure of 10 percent. If homosexuals constitute 10 percent of the total population but commit 33 percent of child molestations, then homosexuals are four times as likely as heterosexuals to engage in child molestation.[2]

And as noted earlier, Kinsey's 10 percent figure is probably overstated. If in fact the percentage of homosexuals is about 2 percent of the total population, then homosexuals are many times more likely to engage in child molestation.

Furthermore, as Knight observes, pedophilia is accepted in part of the homosexual community. The North American Man/Boy Love Association (NAMBLA) actively promotes pedophilia as beneficial to children and adults alike, and regularly marches in Gay Pride parades. Some of the leading homosexual publications, such as the *Advocate*, feature personal ads for prostitution which openly solicit boys.[3] The San Francisco homosexual publication, *Sentinel*, editorialized on 26 March 1992 that "love between men and boys is at the foundation of homosexuality."[4]

We have already noted that homosexuals are three times as likely to have drug and alcohol problems than are heterosexuals. They also have a propensity toward other forms of antisocial behavior. Dr. Frank du Mas, chairman of the Department of Psychology at Augusta College in Georgia, writes:

> Some of the most extensive torture-mass-murders of the twentieth century were performed by homosexual rapists: a Texas engineer, the California Trash Bag murderer, and the Chicago contractor. In these cases, aggression was repeated and premeditated, and it included torture, homosexual rape, mutilation or dismemberment, and murder. In each case there were about thirty murders of boys and young men. Not one older male was a victim.

> I have found no case of a heterosexual equaling this number of murders, and the fact that all of these mass murder incidents included torture and/or dismemberment indicates a higher intensity of aggression.[5]

And finally, Masters and Johnson found that homosexuals were more likely than heterosexuals to have sexual fantasies of force and violence.[6]

I do not suggest that all or even most homosexuals are child abusers, alcoholics, drug abusers, or criminals of other types. But the facts demonstrate that a disproportionate number of homosexuals do engage in these types of behavior.

It is reasonable to assume that crime of various types would increase if homosexuals are allowed into the military. It is also reasonable to assume more child molestation would take place on military outposts. At present most military families regard base housing as a relatively safe place to raise their children. If homosexuals are allowed into the military, base housing may no longer be perceived as safe for children. If the morale of military families collapses, the morale of the armed forces as a whole will likewise be devastated.

Issue #4:
Security Risks

This is the traditional argument against allowing homosexuals in the armed forces: They are security risks. Foreign agents could learn of their homosexuality and use the threat of exposure to blackmail them into compromising national security.

Gay rights advocates argue that this danger is minimal to nonexistent. Now that homosexuality has become more acceptable, the threat of blackmail is reduced considerably. And if the ban is lifted and homosexuals can "come out of the closet," then the threat of blackmail is eliminated because homosexuals will no longer have anything to hide.

These arguments sound convincing, and they may have some merit. Even Secretary of Defense Richard Cheney acknowledged that the homosexual threat to national security is "a bit of an old chestnut."[1]

But lifting the ban would not totally eliminate the blackmail threat. The stigma will remain, at least in some quarters, and many will still want their homosexuality kept secret. As Robert Knight says, "No amount of cultural acceptance of homosexuality will appease a wife who discovers that her husband has been having sex with men."[2]

91

Major Wells-Petry observes that homosexuality is only
one factor in national security.[3] The Ninth Circuit Court
of Appeals observed in *High Tech Gays v. Defense Industrial Security Clearance Office* (1990) that the KGB and
intelligence agencies of other hostile nations instruct
their agents to attempt to

> identify those who are ideologically sympathetic,
> experiencing career difficulties, unsuccessful in social
> relationships, experiencing problems with narcot-
> ics, alcohol, homosexuality, or marital difficul-
> ties. . . . no one trait may be sufficient, and . . .
> the KGB is encouraged when these traits are found
> in combination. . . . The KGB is not primarily
> interested in homosexuals because of their presumed
> susceptibility to blackmail. In its judgment, homo-
> sexuality often is accompanied by personality disor-
> ders that make the victim potentially unstable and
> vulnerable to adroit manipulation.[4]

As Major Wells-Petry explains,

> Thus, some hostile intelligence agencies view
> homosexuality as a marker for other exploitable
> traits. . . .
>
> Disclosure of one's homosexuality does not "immu-
> nize" a soldier from hostile intelligence targeting.
> Indeed, general awareness of one's homosexuality
> might facilitate targeting. Even open homosexuals
> remain vulnerable to coercion based on loyalty to,
> or pressure by, partners who do not want their own
> homosexuality exposed. Moreover, disclosure does
> not preclude the possibility that the presence of
> homosexuals in a military unit will cause increased
> hostile intelligence activity, which is a harm to be
> avoided in its own right.[5]

Especially in conjunction with other factors, homosexuality may be a basis for blackmail, or other means

of compromising national security. There are clearly chinks in the armor of homosexual military personnel targeted by hostile intelligence agencies which do not exist in the profiles of most heterosexual service members. The danger homosexuals pose to national security may not be as substantial as in the past, but it is still a factor to be considered.

Issue #5:
Heterosexual Privacy

With all the attention given to the rights of homosexuals, it is appropriate to consider the rights of heterosexuals as well. One of those rights is the right to privacy. Because American society values privacy, we practice gender segregation in most intimate situations such as sleeping arrangements, shower facilities, and bathrooms.

Major Wells-Petry explains it well:

> Gender segregation is based on two presumptions. The first presumption is that people have a sexual preference for persons of the opposite sex. The second presumption is that people should be allowed to choose to whom, by exposing their bodies or by engaging in intimate bodily functions, they expose an aspect of their sexuality. Since sexuality is not in issue when heterosexuals are segregated by gender, the privacy implications of bodily exposure and intimate bodily functions are not in jeopardy.[1]

She continues,

> Nor do soldiers of either gender deserve to be stripped unwittingly of their right to choose to whom they reveal themselves in a sexual context. Thus,

95

the only way to maintain the protection and discipline—and, as will be seen, public acceptance of and respect for military service—that is otherwise achieved through gender segregation is either to exclude homosexuals or to accommodate them, if possible.[2]

Accommodation simply is not feasible, if for no other reason than that gay rights leaders will not accept segregated status.

General H. Norman Schwarzkopf has voiced a similar objection:

Servicemembers view being forced to sleep, shower, and use toilet facilities with members of the opposite sex as an infringement of their privacy. To force them to live under similar conditions with members of the same sex having a different sexual preference would be a similar infringement of privacy.[3]

Lt. Col. Vickie S. Longenecker offers a refutation of General Schwarzkopf's argument:

Curiously, what DOD's argument implies is that homosexuals are attracted to every other heterosexual. This, of course, is absurd. Think for a moment in terms of heterosexual relationships: Are all men attracted to all women, and all women attracted to all men? Of course not! We are attracted (sexually and otherwise) to people based on our own set of criteria. Homosexuals are no different.[4]

This is a strange argument indeed! One who accepts Lt. Col. Longenecker's reasoning should have no objection to showering with persons of the opposite sex, provided none of those persons is sexually attracted to him or her. The basis of the DOD policy is that when men and women are together in a state of undress, there is at least a substantial possibility that some will regard others as sexual objects, and this constitutes an invasion of privacy. As the Federal District Court for the District of Columbia noted in *Steffan v. Cheney* (1991),

> In the Military Establishment . . . the policy of separating men and women while sleeping, bathing and "using the bathroom" seeks to maintain the privacy of officers and the enlisted while in certain cases of undress. The embarrassment of being naked as between the sexes is prevalent because sometimes the other is considered to be a sexual object. The quite rational assumption in the Navy is that with no one present who has a homosexual orientation, men and women alike can undress, sleep, bathe, and use the bathroom without fear or embarrassment that they are being viewed as sexual objects.[5]

The right not to be viewed as a sexual object while undressing or performing intimate bodily functions is a basic privacy right. Compelling heterosexual men and women to live together would violate that right. Compelling heterosexual men or women to live with homosexuals of the same sex would at least equally violate that right.

Issue #6:
Morale and Discipline

In military jargon, the terms "morale" and "discipline" are often used but seldom defined. *The Random House Dictionary of the English Language* defines morale as the "moral or mental condition with respect to cheerfulness, confidence, zeal, etc.," and discipline as "behavior in accord with rules of conduct; behavior and order maintained by training and control: good discipline in an army."

Morale and discipline are essential to an effective military. As Lt. Col. John F. Guilmartin said, "War is fundamentally a human phenomenon, a matter of emotions, aspirations, exertion, and suffering. Though concrete, physical, and statistical factors obviously play a role in determining conflict's outcome, war ultimately comes down to a contest of knowledge, intelligence, willpower, and human endurance."[1]

Morale and discipline are almost impossible to quantify, but the opinions of military leaders must be considered in determining what undermines morale and discipline. Col. David Hackworth, recipient of eight Purple Hearts and the most decorated living American veteran, says concerning homosexuals in the armed

99

forces, "I cannot think of a better way to destroy fighting spirit and gut U.S. combat effectiveness."[2] Eldon Yates, chairman of the Vietnam Veterans Institute, agrees: "At this point we are in opposition based on the traditional reason, that it is a detriment to mission effectiveness and morale."[3] The objections of Generals Colin Powell and H. Norman Schwarzkopf have already been noted.

S.L.A. Marshall, combat historian for the U.S. Army, conducted four hundred interviews of combat veterans after World War II and concluded that the soldier is motivated to fight primarily by a sense of unity with his combat group:

> I hold it to be one of the simplest truths of war that the thing which enables an infantry soldier to keep going with his weans is the near presence or the presumed presence of a comrade. The warmth which derives from human companionship is as essential to his employment of the arms with which he fights as is the finger with which he pulls a trigger or the eye with which he aligns his sights. . . . So it is far more than a question of the soldier's need of physical support from other men. He must have at least some feeling of spiritual unity with them if he is to do an efficient job of moving and fighting. Should he lack this feeling for any reason . . . he will become a castaway in the middle of a battle and as incapable of effective offensive action as if he were stranded somewhere without weapons.

> This is a basic principle in the elementary psychology of the infantry soldier. Though I have personally investigated several hundred of the heroic exploits by single individuals in the past war . . . I have yet to find the episode which is at odds with it.[4]

So how do homosexuals interfere with this unit bonding?

As Secretary of Defense Richard Cheney says,

> Unit cohesion [is] based on human emotions and relationships . . . are you going to load on to that people who are avowedly gay, publicly and overtly pursuing a gay life-style? That begins to break down unit cohesion.[5]

The secretary's point is that soldiers will hesitate to bond with one another into an effective fighting force if they suspect that others in the unit are motivated by homosexual attraction. One can imagine the difficulties two soldiers will experience working together in combat if one has a reputation for being homosexual, or if the two have had a sexual relationship in the past, or if one has made advances toward the other in the past and been rejected, or if one disapproves of the other's moral standards, or if one fears that the other may carry a contaminating disease. As Col. Hackworth says,

> On the battlefield, what allows men to survive is combat units made up of disciplined team players, who are realistically trained and led by caring skippers who set the example and know their trade. When all of these factors are in synch, a unit has the right stuff. It becomes tight, a family, and clicks like a professional football team. Spirited men who place their lives in their buddies' hands are the most essential element in warfare. The members of such combat teams trust one another totally.
>
> One doesn't need to be a field marshal to understand that sex between service members undermines those critical factors that produce discipline, military orders, spirit and combat effectiveness. Mix boys and girls, gays and straights in close quarters such as the barracks or the battlefield, and both sexual

contact and the consequent breakdown of morale
are inevitable.[6]

Homosexuals in the military could undermine discipline and morale in other ways. Their presence could polarize units, causing antagonism and discord. Col. Hackworth notes,

> In Italy, for example, in the post-war occupation, a gay soldier could not keep his hands off other soldiers in my squad. He disrupted discipline, mangled trust among squad members and zeroed out morale. In the same unit, the personnel major was gay. He had affairs with ambitious teenage soldiers in exchange for kicking up their test scores. This corrupted the command's promotion system and led to the commissioning of William Calley-like lieutenants not fit to lead combat soldiers.
>
> During my second tour in the Korean War, a gay commanding officer gave combat awards to his lovers who had never been on the line. In Vietnam, a young captain in my unit was asked by the commander to go to bed with him. This almost destroyed the esprit of a fine parachute unit.
>
> These are not isolated incidents. During my Army career, I saw countless officers and NCOs who couldn't stop themselves from hitting on soldiers. The absoluteness of their authority, the lack of privacy, enforced intimacy and a 24-hour duty day made sexual urges difficult to control. The objects of their affection were impressionable lads who, searching for a caring role model, sometimes ended up in a gay relationship they might not have sought.[7]

In a similar vein, Kevin M. McCrane describes his World War II experience aboard the *U.S.S. Warrick*:

> There were five such aggressive homosexuals that we knew of on board this ship with almost 250 men. They were all petty officers. Their actions were

enough to poison the atmosphere on the *Warrick*. Meals, showers, attendance at the movies, decisions about where you went on the ship alone—all became part of a worried calculation of risk.

After two weeks at sea, I received the whispered news that the smallest and most vulnerable of our "team" had been sodomized in the paint locker. When I looked at the bearer of this news, I saw that there were tears in his eyes. "Why are they doing this to us?" he asked.

It was a good question. The comments of some petty officers suggested that the rapid discharge of so many veterans at the end of the war had brought with it a slackening of discipline. On board the *Warrick* this disciplinary neglect had loosened the restraints on homosexual behavior—the threat of discharge was the surest of these—and created an atmosphere where exhibitionism and lewd action were commonplace.

All homosexuals aren't rapists. But in this closed male society, with its enforced communal living, unchecked homosexual appetites wrought havoc. The atmosphere on the *USS Warrick* in January of 1946 does have a present-day parallel—the atmosphere of fear that rules in today's prisons.

Is there a lesson here for Mr. Clinton? I think so. The U.S. Navy certainly won't turn into a collection of horror ships like the *Warrick* if he succeeds in ending the ban on homosexuals in the military. But my experience does suggest that military officials are right to worry that "good order and discipline of the services will be impaired" if the ban is lifted.[8]

Col. William A. Woodruff, a law professor at Campbell University, has observed that

junior personnel, particularly recruits, are vulnerable to abuse, including unwanted sexual advances

by those in authority. A 1990 report by the Navy
Women's Study Group concluded that "junior
women feel intimidated when homosexuality is
suspected or present in their command and there
are indications that some have been victimized by
lesbian harassment." The study observed that junior
women lack the experience, maturity, and confidence
needed to combat the problem effectively. They
expressed fear of retaliation from what is perceived
as an alliance of lesbians. This fear inhibits their
reporting harassment and cooperating with investi-
gations.[9]

Besides causing discord within units, homosexuality
could undermine respect for authority. Soldiers might
have great difficulty respecting and obeying a homosexual officer, especially if that officer has made sexual
advances toward them or is perceived as having shown
favoritism toward those who accept his advances.

Is homosexuality compatible with military discipline?
Apparently some homosexuals don't think so. In the
past, many have shunned the military as contrary to
their basic nonmilitaristic and nonaggressive values. As
noted earlier, on 9 January 1993 I attended a workshop
on the military exclusion of homosexuals sponsored by
the Association of American Law Schools (AALS). One
of the speakers was Mary Newcombe, staff attorney for
the LAMBDA Legal Defense and Education Fund, the
nation's leading pro-homosexual legal defense organization. Ms. Newcombe has represented numerous homosexuals in cases against the armed forces. She told the
workshop participants:

> The question that I kept getting from the gay com-
> munity in particular was, why would we want to
> promote militarism in society? Isn't militarism di-
> rectly opposed to a progressive liberation movement?

> Well, first of all, I think it is absolutely right that
> the gay rights movement in its fundamental heart
> is a very radical movement, and sexual liberation is
> an important component of that movement, as well
> as a progressive agenda is a very important part of
> that movement, 'cause it's radicalizing, and the Right
> Wing is absolutely right, it is radicalizing the family,
> and it is radicalizing the way we look at American
> society.[10]

After suggesting several reasons why homosexuals
might want to enter military service, Ms. Newcombe
went on to say,

> So will the increased presence of women and gay
> people in the military decrease militarism? I don't
> know if you know Mary Dunlap; she's done a lot
> of work on this issue, but Mary swears that that's
> the reason why she's worked on this issue for so
> long; _she absolutely believes that ultimately we'll change_
> _the militarism and change the aggressiveness of the_
> _military; and I very much hope she's right._[11] (Emphasis
> mine.)

Let us focus on the significance of this statement.
An attorney for the nation's leading pro-homosexual legal
defense organization openly acknowledges that a primary reason for working to get homosexuals into the
armed forces is to "change the aggressiveness of the
military." Having acknowledged that as a primary goal,
it would seem difficult to argue that the presence of
homosexuals will not affect military discipline or hinder
the military mission of winning the nation's wars.

As General Colin L. Powell has noted,

> The judgment in our courts over time has been
> [that] the presumption has to be on someone else
> [to prove] that the introduction of such a new
> element would not be detrimental to good order
> and discipline.[12]

General Powell's point is that on a matter as crucial as the defense of the nation, the burden of proof must rest on those who wish to change military policy. The burden should not rest upon the military to prove that lifting the gay ban would adversely affect the armed forces. Rather, those who want to admit homosexuals in the military have to prove that this change would not adversely affect military discipline and thereby jeopardize the nation's defense.

Those who want to end the gay ban have not met this burden of proof. In fact, the evidence is strongly to the contrary. By disturbing and preventing unit bonding, creating an atmosphere of fear and distrust, causing discord within units, and undermining respect for authority, the presence of homosexuals in the military would be prejudicial to the good order and discipline of the armed forces.

10

Issue #7:
Problems of Implementation

For the reasons given earlier, plus the overwhelming opposition among current military personnel, integrating homosexuals into the military will be difficult to accomplish.

Proponents argue that the task is similar to that of integrating blacks into the armed forces after World War II. Lt. McIntyre says education will be the key, and it should be accomplished through workshops. Lt. McIntyre suggests one such workshop sponsored by the National Sex Forum, another used by the San Francisco Police Department, and still another offered by the medical center at the University of California in San Francisco. The last of these, he says approvingly,

> includes a series of seminars on gay relationships as well as first-hand experience with gay individuals, couples and families. Students form same-sex pairs, eat at a gay restaurant, go drinking and dancing at gay night spots and then later the same night meet to discuss their experiences.[1]

A recently-leaked memo by the Gay, Lesbian, and Bisexual Military Freedom Project recommends that the armed forces

A. Institute training for all personnel on the acceptance of homosexual or bisexual personnel into the
military. Training shall include didactic and expe-
riential opportunities addressing prejudice, stigma,
and discrimination with regard to sexual orientation and be based on experience gained dealing
with racial and gender issues. Training programs
needed include, but are not limited to the following: (1) Individual, Unit, Service Schools and Acad-
emies. (2) Chaplains and the Medical Corps. (3)
Law enforcement and investigative agencies. (4)
Sexual orientation with regards to sexual harassment
and equal opportunity.

B. Expand mission of Defense Equal Opportunity
Management Institute to include issues related to
sexual orientation discrimination.[2]

A workshop like this is likely to meet with much
resistance among military personnel. Unlike racial discrimination, which is based upon fear and prejudice,
objections to homosexuality are based upon sincere
religious and moral convictions and upon sound, rational
evidence.

Will commanders be required to "educate" their
troops on the subject? If so, what will they be required
to say? Will they have to affirm that homosexuality is
an acceptable life-style? Commanders and high-ranking
civilian employees of various branches of the service
have told me they would resign from the service rather
than compromise their convictions by affirming that
which they know to be wrong.

What if homosexuals are allowed in the military but
Article 125 of the Uniform Code of Military Justice
remains in effect and thus homosexual acts are forbidden? Is it feasible, even realistic, to expect most homosexuals to remain celibate? It seems unlikely.

And many other questions arise. What would happen, for example, if an unmarried Air Force man and woman wanted to live together on base in the barracks? With some justification they could argue that homosexual lovers are allowed to live together. Would the armed forces countenance homosexual living arrangements but deny heterosexuals the same privilege?

What if a heterosexual soldier objects to sharing a room with a homosexual? Will his or her preference be honored? Does he have a right to know his roommate's orientation, considering that his own health may be in jeopardy?

Would the armed forces recognize homosexual marriages? If a homosexual soldier married a civilian of the same sex, would they be entitled to collect Basic Allowance for Quarters (BAQ) and subsistence? Would his "spouse" be entitled to base privileges such as hospital, base exchange, commissary, etc.?

Would homosexual couples be allowed to live in base housing? What if next door neighbors with small children object? How will this affect morale among servicemen and their families? Will military families continue to regard base housing as a safe and wholesome place to raise their children?

What about "affirmative action?" Michael Petrelis, a veteran gay activist, is calling for homosexual quotas in the military.[3] Will this be honored?

And what about military chaplains? Will a chaplain be allowed to preach his conviction that homosexual conduct is contrary to the Word of God? Must he administer the sacraments to one who he believes is living in sin? Does this not raise First Amendment issues of free exercise of religion and free speech?

What about military auxiliaries like the Civil Air Patrol, which includes youths age thirteen and older and which commonly meets on military bases or Guard armories. Will they be forced to admit homosexuals? If they do not, will they be denied access to military bases? And most military bases have other organizations that meet on base, such as the Boy Scouts. Will these groups be allowed to exist and meet on base if they do not admit homosexuals?

The Army and Air National Guard units raise an entirely different set of legal and constitutional issues. Guard units are normally under the control of state officials (the Ohio National Guard, etc.) unless they are ordered into federal service by the President or Congress. If the gay ban is lifted for active duty forces, will Guard units be required to include homosexuals as well? What will happen if state officials refuse to do so?

These are only a few of the complex legal, ethical, and practical difficulties that will arise if homosexuals are allowed into the armed forces.

The "Status/Conduct" Distinction and Pending Action

On 29 January 1993, President Clinton announced that the secretary of defense will draw up a new policy on homosexuals in the armed forces not later than July 1993. In the meantime, he said, recruiters will no longer ask potential enlistees about their sexual orientation, most discharges based solely on sexual orientation will be at least temporarily suspended, and certain soldiers whose proposed discharges are pending review will be placed in the standby reserve until the policy changes are completed. In the meantime, as of this writing, Congress plans to hold hearings on the issue in March 1993. In response to widespread public opposition the President emphasized that at least for the present he was insisting only that persons should not be discharged or be denied enlistment solely because of their status or orientation as homosexuals; conduct may be another matter.

In my view, the so-called "status/conduct" distinction cannot be maintained in the long run. Homosexual orientation leads to homosexual conduct just as surely as heterosexual orientation leads to heterosexual conduct. (And, no, I do not expect most heterosexual soldiers to remain celibate; that's why we have the institution of marriage.)

The idea that homosexuals will be content to refrain from homosexual acts if they are allowed to enter the military is hardly realistic. Some individual homosexuals might; but the militant gay rights leaders will never settle for that. They will argue, "By admitting us into the armed forces, you have already accepted our orientation as legitimate. How can you then deny us the right to engage in homosexual conduct that is as natural for us as heterosexual conduct is for you? So long as you deny us the same right to engage in homosexual conduct that heterosexuals have to engage in heterosexual conduct, you are treating us as second class soldiers and second class citizens." In fact, a recently-leaked memo by a leading gay and lesbian task force openly stated their intent to do exactly that as soon as the new order is in effect.

I am therefore of the opinion that the so-called status/conduct distinction represents nothing more than a halfway house to full acceptance of homosexual conduct.

11

Conclusions
and
Recommendations

The contradictory claims of the homosexual lobby are confusing. They argue that the military ban costs the armed forces extensive manpower, but in the next breath they claim the ban is unenforceable, that homosexuals are already serving in proportionate numbers, and the only real issue is not whether they will serve but whether they will serve legally and openly.

They say they don't want to be identified by their sexual orientation, but they demand special recognition as a minority group and insist that except for their sexual orientation they are just like everyone else.

They claim to be a persecuted minority, yet in the next breath they claim overwhelming public support. They plead that their sexual orientation is something innate over which they have no control, yet they assure us they can control their urges and pose no threat to heterosexuals.

We are asked to believe homosexuals are just as capable soldiers as heterosexuals, yet some of them claim the real reason they want to enter the armed forces is to break down the military's aggressiveness and decrease militarism. They assure us they are no threat to children, yet some of them argue that children should be free to engage in homosexual relations even with adults.

And gay activists insist the way to eliminate prejudice against homosexuals is to educate the public about homosexuality; yet they are outraged when the graphic details about homosexual practices and health hazards are presented.

Based upon the information and ideas presented in this paper, what other conclusions can be drawn but the following?

- DOD policy prohibits homosexual acts and prohibits those with homosexual tendencies from serving in the armed forces.
- This policy deters homosexuals from entering military service but does not entirely keep them out; it deters service members from engaging in homosexual acts but does not completely prevent them from taking place. While not completely effective, the policy's deterrent effect is substantial.
- This policy is currently facing several court challenges but will almost certainly be upheld as constitutional by the U.S. Supreme Court.
- Contrary to the inflated Kinsey figures, the percentage of the population that is homosexual is probably about 2 percent. The percentage in the armed forces is probably no higher than that, and probably lower because of the deterrent effect of DOD policy.
- Western civilization has traditionally regarded homosexuality as immoral because it is contrary to the Bible, contrary to the natural order, and involves many practices that the majority find vile and offensive.

- While the causes of homosexuality are still in dispute or unknown, there is much evidence that many homosexuals can and do convert or revert to heterosexuality.
- Homosexuals have a much higher incidence of AIDS, venereal disease, and other diseases, as well as alcohol, drug, and emotional problems and a greatly shortened life expectancy of forty-one years. They therefore pose a health hazard for themselves and other military personnel which would be costly in terms of money, manpower, and the human tragedy involved.
- Homosexuals have a high incidence of pedophilia and certain other crimes and other types of antisocial behavior.
- Homosexuals constitute a security risk; public acknowledgment of homosexuality does not eliminate that risk.
- The integration of homosexuals into the armed forces would violate the privacy rights of heterosexuals to dress, undress, and perform intimate bodily functions without being viewed as sex objects.
- The presence of homosexuals would prevent military units from bonding, polarize units, create an atmosphere of fear and distrust, and undermine respect for authority, and would therefore jeopardize the good order and discipline of the armed forces. Certain spokespersons for the homosexual community have openly acknowledged that their goal is to rid the armed forces of their "aggressiveness" and "militarism."
- The integration of homosexuals into the armed forces in the face of sincere religious and moral objections of the vast majority of servicemembers would be

difficult to implement and would involve many serious problems concerning the rights of homosexuals and heterosexuals to military housing, military entitlements, chaplain services, Guard units, etc.

- Admitting homosexuals into the armed forces and segregating them into separate units, or barring them from leadership or combat, is not feasible in that homosexuals would refuse to accept such status.

Further, based upon these conclusions, I offer the following recommendations:

- That the current DOD directive forbidding homosexuality in the armed forces be retained in essence.
- That a study commission be created to study the feasibility of allowing certain former homosexuals to enter the armed forces and allowing certain present or former homosexuals to remain in the armed forces. Since considerable evidence indicates that a large percentage of homosexuals can convert or revert to heterosexuality, especially if they strongly desire to do so, they should if possible be given that opportunity. The armed forces could establish a program similar to the Limited Privileged Communication Program which the Air Force operated for drug abusers during the 1970s. The individual could report to an internal department overseeing social actions, acknowledge his homosexuality, and have his admission treated with complete confidentiality. He could then be given a program of therapy to convert or revert to heterosexuality. If, upon completion of the program, a military psychologist or psychiatrist certifies that he has been cured of homosexuality and is unlikely to revert to homosexuality in the future, and if the member himself affirms that he has no intention of engaging in future

homosexual behavior, he may be retained in the armed forces and his past homosexuality and treatment would be kept confidential. If a cure cannot be effected, he would be honorably discharged. The person desiring to enter the armed forces would, upon similar completion of treatment and certification by a mental health professional, be allowed to enlist.

With this change, no one need be barred from military service because of past homosexuality. At the same time, no one need fear homosexuals in the military in the future.

A Closing Word

It is clear from this study that I believe homosexuality to be morally wrong, a hazard to health, and a detriment to the good order and discipline of the armed forces. However, I hold no personal animosity toward homosexuals.

One of the most encouraging elements of this rather sober study is the abundant evidence that homosexuals can change, particularly if they are motivated to do so. It is my hope that the hard data presented in this study will persuade homosexuals to seek help and escape from a life-style that is in fact a death-style.

U.S. Senator Daniel Patrick Moynihan (D-NY) said it well:

> I proffer the thesis that over the past generation the amount . . . of deviant behavior in American society has increased beyond the levels the community can "afford to recognize" and that, accordingly, we have been redefining deviancy so as to exempt much conduct previously stigmatized, and also quietly raising the "normal" level in categories where behavior is now abnormal by an earlier standard.[1]

. . . and Sun Tzu wrote in *The Art of War* (approximately 5th century B.C.):

> The consummate leader cultivates the moral law, and strictly adheres to method and discipline, thus it is in his power to control success.[2]

Appendix

Gays in Uniform: A Survey of Current Literature on the Subject

Much has been written about homosexuality in general; since this book concentrates upon the issue of homosexuals and the military, this appendix will focus on the literature addressing the same. A substantial body of such literature exists, much of it by military personnel; and some of this literature supports inclusion of homosexuals in the armed forces.

Among the best literature supporting the inclusion of homosexuals in the armed forces is the 1980 Naval Postgraduate School master's thesis of Navy Lt. Michael T. McIntyre, "Homosexuality and the U.S. Military." The thesis is 133 pages in length, well-written, well-reasoned, and well-documented. Unfortunately, Lt. McIntyre naively accepts the misleading 10 percent homosexual figure attributed to Kinsey, and this colors many of his conclusions.[1]

"Facts or Fear from the Foxhole" is the 1992 program paper for the U.S. Army War College by Lt. Col. Vickie S. Longenecker. In her abstract Lt. Col.

Longenecker claims that her study "examines all sides of the argument in an unbiased and objective manner,"[2] but in fact her paper is a strident diatribe for gay rights. She opens by describing those who oppose having homosexuals in the military as "voices of fear, prejudice, and hatred" and describes attempts to remove homosexuals as "witch-hunts."[3] This is a standard tactic of gay rights advocates. They describe their positions as open-minded, tolerant, and factual and caricature their opponents as narrow-minded bigots who can support their positions with nothing but fear, hatred, and prejudice. She even suggests that opponents of gay rights are motivated by their own fear of "sexual inadequacy."[4]

Lt. Col. Longenecker quotes the DOD policy on homosexuality cited above, then states flatly, "However, there is absolutely no recorded empirical data to support this long-standing policy."[5] Such a statement, to put the best possible construction on Lt. Col. Longenecker's motives, reflects an abysmal ignorance of the facts.

Lt. Col. Longenecker declares that "the average American regards homosexuals with fear and loathing."[6] But later she cites polls suggesting that a strong majority of Americans support gay rights, and she chides the Department of Defense for failure to keep pace with public opinion.[7] Such strident rhetoric, inconsistent reasoning, among other fallacies exposed earlier in this book, greatly diminish the scholarship and credibility of her work.

In May 1976 two papers were presented to the Air Command and Staff College, "The Homosexual in Uniform" by Major Billy F. Lacy, and "The Homosexual Challenge" by Major Dean A. Johnson. Both support the inclusion of homosexuals in the military. In a similar vein, in 1983 Army Captain James E. Foley presented a paper to the Armed Forces Staff College titled "Updating the Policy Barring Homosexuals." All three papers are reasonably well-done, of less value than that of Lt. McIntyre but above that of Lt. Col. Longenecker.[8]

In June 1992 the General Accounting Office (GAO) released a report titled "Defense Force Management: DOD's Policy on Homosexuality" at the request of avowed homosexual Representative Gerry E. Studds (D-Mass) and two other congressmen, Representatives John Conyers, Jr. (D-Mich), and Ted Weiss (D-NY).[9] The paper is valuable for its documentation and tables of statistics; its inclusion of a lengthy statement of objections by the Department of Defense is also helpful. The paper concludes that DOD's policy of excluding homosexuals should be eliminated. Surprisingly (or perhaps not so), the report avoids the issue of Acquired Immune Deficiency Syndrome (AIDS) and its effect if homosexuality is legalized. Clearly, the question of whether allowing homosexuals into the armed forces would increase the spread of AIDS among military personnel and dependents deserves to be addressed.

In 1971 Colin J. Williams and Martin S. Weinberg released a book entitled *Homosexuals and the Military* (New York: Harper & Row), which aids in understanding the effects of less-than-honorable discharges upon homosexuals but which does not address the basic issues of this book. Likewise, Mary Ann Humphrey's *My Country, My Right to Serve* (New York: Harper Collins, 1990), mentioned in chapter 1, and *Get Off My Ship: Ensign Berg vs. the U.S. Navy* (New York: Avon, 1978) provide insight into the personal dilemmas of homosexuals in the military.

On the other side of the issue, "The Power to Raise and Support Armies: The Homosexual Exclusion Policy in Perspective," submitted by Army Captain (now Major) Melissa Wells-Petry,[10] is outstanding. Her paper is 355 pages in length, and in order to get the full force and effect of the paper it is necessary to read it in its entirety, especially the 520 endnotes which contain some of the paper's most salient information. I found Major Wells-Petry's medical documentation especially helpful.

Commander Eugene T. Gomulka, assistant chief of chaplains of the Marine Corps, has prepared a brief but hard-hitting paper titled "Position Paper on the DOD Policy on Homosexuality,"[11] which is well-documented and contains valuable information and insight.

Other literature supporting current military policy includes "Should the Military's Ban on Homosexuals Be Lifted?"—prepared in November 1992 by Robert H. Knight of the Family Research Council. Knight and the Family Research Council have also prepared "Sexual Disorientation: Faulty Research in the Homosexual Debate" (June 1992) and "How Lifting the Military Homosexual Ban May Affect Families" (November 1992).[12] "Homosexuals in the Military," a text of testimony before a Republican Research Committee hearing by Congressman William E. Dannemeyer (R-CA),[13] and two articles from *Psychological Reports* by Dr. Paul Cameron, Dr. Kirk Cameron, and Dr. Kay Proctor, entitled "Effect of Homosexuality upon Public Health and Social Order"[14] and "Homosexuals in the Armed Forces"[15] are also helpful. The first Cameron article in particular provides valuable information about the unusual practices associated with homosexuality.

Notes

Introduction

1. General Douglas MacArthur quoted by John, A. Stormer, *The Death of a Nation* (Florissant, Mo.: Liberty Bell Press, 1968), 23.

2. David Horowitz, "The Queer Fellows," *American Spectator* (January 1993): 42.

3. Major R. D. Adair and Captain Joseph C. Myers, "Admission of Gays to the Military: A Singularly Intolerant Act," *Parameters: U.S. Army War College Quarterly* XXIII (Spring 1993): 10-19, 17.

Chapter 1: What is Homosexuality?

1. Alfred C. Kinsey et. al., *Sexual Behavior in the Human Male* (Philadelphia: W.B. Saunders & Co., 1948), 639.

2. Ibid., 650-651.

3. Alfred C. Kinsey et. al., *Sexual Behavior in the Human Female* (Philadelphia: W.B. Saunders & Co., 1953), 474-475.

4. Dr. Judith A. Reisman and Edward W. Eichel, *Kinsey, Sex and Fraud: The Indoctrination of a People* (Lafayette, LA: Lochinvar/Huntington House, 1990), 17, 20, 62, 181.

5. Ibid., 23.

6. Ibid., 63-64.

7. Ibid., 39-40.

8. Ibid., 21, 63-73, et. al.

9. Gary Ramafedi, "Demography of Sexual Orientation in Adolescents," *Pediatrics* 89 (1992): 714-721.

10. Tom W. Smith, "Adult Sexual Behavior in 1989: Number of Partners, Frequency of Intercourse and Risk of AIDS," *Family Planning Perspectives* (May/June 1991): 102.

11. D. Forman and C. Chilvers, "Sexual Behavior of Young and Middle-Aged Men in England and Wales," *British Medical Journal* 298 (29 April 1989): 1137-1142.

12. Dr. Paul Cameron, *Family Research Report* (October-December 1991): 2.

13. Congressman William E. Dannemeyer (R-CA), "Homosexuals in the Military" (Testimony before a Republican Research Committee hearing, 9 December 1992): 3. In addition to these cited sources, Congressman Dannemeyer cites Deborah Dawson, "AIDS Knowledge and Attitudes for January-March 1990, Provisional Data from the National Health Interview Survey;" Joseph E. Fitti and Marcie Cynamon, op. cit. for July-September 1990, in *Advance Date*, Nos. 193, 195, 198, National Center for Health Statistics, Centers for Disease Control, Public Health Service, and the U.S. Department of Health and Human Services.

14. "Defense Force Management: DOD's Policy on Homosexuality" *United States General Accounting Office Report to Congressional Requesters, GAO/NSIAD-92-98* (12 June 1992): 60 (hereafter cited as "GAO").

15. Sigmund Freud, "9 April 1935 Letter to the Mother of a Homosexual," reproduced in *Medical Aspects of Human Sexuality* (December 1968): 40.

16. *GAO*, 36.

17. Ibid.

18. Alan P. Bell and Martin S. Weinberg, *Homosexualities: A Study of Diversity Among Men and Women* (New York: Simon & Schuster, 1978), 308.

19. Dr. David D. Ostrow, M.D., Ph.D., and Norman Altman, M.S., "Sexually Transmitted Diseases and Homosexuality," *Sexually Transmitted Diseases* 10 (1983): 208-215.

20. Dr. Anne C. Collier, "Cytomegalovirus Infection in Homosexual Men: Relation to Sexual Practices, Antibody to Human Immunodeficiency Virus and Cell-Mediated Immunity, *American Journal of Medicine* 82 (1987): 593-601.

21. Dr. Mary E. Guinan, M.D., Ph.D., et. al., "Heterosexual and Homosexual Patients with the Acquired Immunodeficiency Syndrome," *Annals of Internal Medicine* 100 (1984): 213-218.

22. Dr. Jonathan W. M. Gold, M.D., "Unexplained Persistent Lymphadenopathy in Homosexual Men and the Acquired Immune Deficiency Syndrome," *Medicine* 64 (1985): 203-213.

23. Dr. Paul Cameron, Dr. Kirk Cameron, and Dr. Kay Proctor, "Effect of Homosexuality upon Public Health and Social Order," *Psychological Reports* 64 (1989): 1167-1179.

24. Ibid., 1171.

25. Ibid.

26. Guinan, "Heterosexual and Homosexual Patients," 213-218.

27. Dr. Walter E. Stamm, et. al., "The Association Between Genital Ulcer Disease and Acquisition of HIV Infection in Homosexual Men," *Journal of the American Medical Association* 260 (9 September 1988): 1429-1433.

Chapter 2: Current Department of Defense Policy on Homosexuality

1. Alfred C. Kinsey, *Sexual Behavior in the Human Female* (Philadelphia: W. B. Saunders Co., 1953), 639.

2. *GAO*, 39.

3. "Fast Track: Quick Updates on the Major Issues," *Air Force Times* (28 December 1992): 16.

Chapter 3: A Response to Arguments for Lifting the Gay Ban

1. Mary Ann Humphries, *My Country, My Right to Serve* (New York: Harper Collins, 1990), xvii.

2. Bolling v Sharpe, 347 U.S. 497 (1954).

3. Bowers v Hardwick, 478 U.S. 186 (1986), also cited Palo v Connecticut, 302 U.S. 319, 325, 326, 58 S.Ct. 149, 151, 152 (1937); Moore v Cleveland, 431 U.S. 494, 97 S.Ct. 1932, 1937 (1977) opinion of J. Powell and 503, 97 S.Ct at 1938 (1977) opinion of J. Powell; see also Griswold v Connecticut, 381 U.S. at 506, 85 S.Ct. at 1693.

4. Goldman v Weinberger, 475 U.S. 503, 106 S.Ct 1310 (1986); Greer v Spock, 424 U.S. 828, 96 S.Ct 1211 (1976).

5. Matlovich v Secretary of the Air Force, 591 F. 2d 852 (D.C. Cir. 1978).

6. Watkins v U.S. Army, 875 F. 2d 699 (1989), cert. den. 111 S.Ct. 384 (1990).

7. Dronenburg v Zech, 741 F. 2d 1388 (D.C. Cir. 1984).

8. Ben-Shalom v Marsh, 881 F. 2d 454 (1988), cert. den. 110 S.Ct. 1296 (1990).

9. Pruitt v Cheney, 943 F. 2d 989 (1991).

10. Mary Newcombe, lecture/response to questions at workshop entitled "Excluding Lesbians and Gay Men from Military Service: Whither the Policy, Whither the AALS," Gay and Lesbian Legal Issues Committee, annual meeting of the Association of American Law Schools (AALS), San Francisco, CA, 9 January 1993; I was present to hear her lecture, which is also available on cassette through the AALS.

11. Kate Dyer, lecture at AALS workshop.

12. Meinhold v Department of Defense, No. CV 92-6044 TJH (JRX), 1993 WL 15899 (C.O. Cal.).

13. Gen. Colin L. Powell, "Powell 'Gays in Military, Farmore Complicated Issue'" *Air Force Times* (14 December 1992): 12.

14. David Horowitz, "The Queer Fellows," *American Spectator* (January 1993): 43.

15. Ibid., 45.

16. Dr. Simon LeVay, "A Difference in Hypothalmic Structure between Heterosexual and Homosexual Men," *Science* 258 (1991): 1034-1037.

17. Robert Knight, "Sexual Disorientation: Faulty Research in the Homosexual Debate" (Family Research Council, Washington, D.C., June 1992): 3-5.

18. Dr. Paul Cameron, "What Causes Homosexual Desire and Can It Be Changed?" (Washington, D.C.: Family Research Institute, 1992); see also Knight, "Sexual Disorientation," 5; Congressman William C. Dannemeyer (R-CA) "Homosexuals in the Military" (Testimony before a Republican Research Committee hearing, 9 December 1992): 4-7.

19. Cameron, "What Causes Homosexual Desire."

20. William H. Masters and Virginia E. Johnson, *Homosexuality in Perspective* (Boston: Little, Brown & Co., 1979), 274-378.

21. Abigail Van Buren, "Dear Abby," *Montgomery Advertiser* (3 January 1993): 3E.

22. Bowers v Hardwick, 478 U.S. 186 (1986).

23. Lt. Col. Vickie S. Longenecker, "Facts or Fear from the Foxhole" (Military Studies Program paper, U.S. Army War College, Carlisle Baracks, PA, 15 April 1992), 8-9.

24. Colin J. Williams and Martin S. Weinberg, *Homosexuals and the Military* (New York: Harper & Row, 1971).

25. Telephone interview with representative of Office of Separations, Maxwell AFB, Montgomery, AL, 26 January 93.

26. "Defense Force Management: DOD's Policy on Homosexuality," *United States General Accounting Office Report to Congressional Requesters, GAO/NS/AD-92-98* (12 June 1992): 65.

27. Ibid., 25.

28. Department of Defense response to GAO Report, 67-68.

29. Horowitz, "The Queer Fellows," 45.

Chapter 4: Issue #1: Against Admitting Homosexuals into the Armed Forces: The Moral Issue

1. This writer has thoroughly documented the Judeo-Christian heritage of this nation in two of his books, *Columbus and Cortez, Conquerors for Christ* (Green Forest, AR: New Leaf Press, 1992) and *Christianity and the Constitution: The Faith of Our Founding Fathers* (Grand Rapids, MI: Baker Book House, 1987, 1991). To avoid repetition, the reader is referred to the documentation in those books.

2. Lt. Col. Vickie S. Longenecker, "Facts or Fear from the Foxhole" (Military Studies Program paper, U.S. Army War College, Carlisle Barracks, PA, 15 April 1992): 13-14.

3. W. Cleon Skousen, *The Miracle of America Study Guide* (Salt Lake City, Utah: National Center for Constitutional Studies, 1981), 20.

4. Major Billy F. Lacy, "The Homosexual in Uniform," (Research study paper, Air Command and Staff College, Air University, Maxwell AFB, Montgomery, AL, May 1976), 8-9.

5. Will Durant and Ariel Durant, *The Story of Civilization II* (New York: Simon & Schuster, 1939, 1966): 48, 83, 149, 301-302, 567.

6. Ibid., III: 89, 369.

7. Ibid., III: 168, 276-82.

8. Ibid., III: 290.

9. Ibid., III: 445.

10. Ibid., III: 94.

11. Ibid., III: 144.

12. Bowers v Hardwick, 106 S.Ct. 2841 (1986) at 2846.

13. Paris Adult Theatre v Slaton, 413 U.S. 49 (1973).

14. Lord Justice Patrick Devlin, *The Enforcement of Morals* (New York: Oxford University Press, 1965), 13ff.

15. Harris v McRae, 448 U.S. 297 (1980).

16. Church of the Holy Trinity v United States, 143 U.S. 457 (1982).

17. Late Corporation of the Church of Jesus Christ of Latter Day Saints v United States, 136 U.S. 1 (1890).

18. Davis v Beason, 133 U.S. 333 (1890).

19. Stone v Mississippi, 101 U.S. 814; Champion v Ames, 188 U.S. 321 (1903).

20. General John A. Lejeune quoted by Commander Eugene T. Gomulka, Deputy Chaplain, U.S. Marine Corps, "Position Paper on the DOD Policy on Homosexuality" (25 July 1992), 6.

Chapter 5: Issue #2: The Health Issue

1. National Center for Infectious Diseases, Division of HIV/AIDS, Centers for Disease Control, "The HIV/AIDS Surveillance Report" (January 1992): 9.

2. Dr. Charles Davis, Dean of Academic Affairs, Air War College, and Professor of Statistics, Southwest Texas State University, statistical computations explained and verified in telephone conversation 26 January 93.

3. Robert Knight, "Sexual Disorientation: Family Research in the Homosexual Debate" (Family Research Council, Washington, D.C., June 1992), 6.

4. Dr. Jonathan W. M. Gold, M. D., "Unexplained Persistent Lymphadenopathy in Homosexual Men and the Acquired Immune Deficiency Sydrome," *Medicine* 64 (1985): 204.

5. Dr. Robert S. Ernst, M.D., and Dr. Peter S. Houts, Ph.D., "Characteristics of Gay Persons with Sexually Transmitted Diseases," *Sexually Transmitted Diseases* 12 (1985):59-63.

6. Dr. Anne C. Collier, "Cytomegalovirus Infection in Homosexual Men: Relation to Sexual Practices, Antibody to Human Immunodeficiency Virus and Cell-Mediated Immunity, *American Journal of Medicine* 82 (1987): 594.

7. Dr. Miriam J. Alter, "Hepatitis B Virus Transmission Between Heterosexuals," *Journal of the American Medical Association* 256 (1986): 1307-1310.

8. Alan P. Bell and Martin S. Weinberg, *Homosexualities: A Study of Diversity about Men and Women* (New York: Simon & Schuster, 1978), 308.

9. Dr. Paul Cameron, Dr. Kirk Cameron, and Dr. Kay Proctor, "Effect of Homosexuality upon Public Health and Social Order," *Psychological Reports* 64 (1989): 1167-1179; Dr. Mary Guinan, M.D., Ph.D., et al., "Heterosexual and Homosexual Patients with the Acquired Immunodeficiency Syndrome," *Annals of Internal Medicine* 100 (1984): 213-218; Dr. Walter E. Stamm, et al., "The Association between Genital Ulcer Disease and Acquisition of HIV Infection in Homosexual Men," *Journal of the American Medical Association* 260 (9 September 1988): 1429-1433.

10. Ibid.

11. Dr. Lode Wigersma, "Safety and Acceptability of Condoms for Use by Homosexual Men as a Prophylactic against Transmission of HIV During Anogenital Sexual Intercourse," *British Medical Journal* 295 (11 July 1987): 94.

12. Dr. Christian Goilav, M.D., and Dr. Peter Piot, M.D., "Vaccination Against Hepatitis B in Homosexual Men," *American Journal of Medicine* 87 (1989): 3A-21S–3A-25S.

13. Dr. James E. Barone, "Management of Foreign Bodies and Trauma of the Rectum," *Surgery, Gynecology and Obstetrics* 156 (1983): 453-457.

14. Dr. Alexander Kingsley, M.D. and Dr. Herand Abcarian, M.D., "Colorectal Foreign Bodies, Management Update," *Diseases of the Colon and Rectum* 28 (1986): 941-944.

15. Dr. Irving B. Margolis, "Sexually Transmitted Anal and Rectal Infections," *Surgery, Gynecology and Obstetrics* 161 (August 1985): 42.

16. Barone, "Management of Foreign Bodies," 453-457.

17. Dr. L. Gottesman, M.D., et. al.,"The Use of Water-Soluble Contrast Enemas in the Diagnosis of Acute Lower Left Quadrant Peritonitis," _Diseases of the Colon and Rectum_ 27 (1984): 84-88.

18. Barone, "Management of Foreign Bodies," 453-457.

19. Dr. Elizabeth A. Holly, "Anal Cancer Incidents: Genital Warts, Anal Fissure or Fistula, Hemorrhoids, and Smoking," _Journal of the National Cancer Institute_ 11 (1989): 1726-1732.

20. Dr. J. Hampton Atkinson, MD, et. al., "Prevalence of Psychiatric Disorders Among Men Infected with [HIV]," _Archives of General Psychiatry_ 45 (September 1988): 859-864.

21. Dr. Chris Anne Raymond, Ph.D., "Addressing Homosexuals' Mental Health Problems," _Journal of the American Medical Association_ 259 (1 January 1988): 19.

22. Martin S. Weinberg and Colin J. Williams, _Male Homosexuals_ (1974), cited by S. Goldberg, "Is Homosexuality Normal?", _Policy Review_ 21 (Summer 1982): 119-127.

23. "Gays Are More Prone to Substance Abuse," _Insight_ (5 November 1990): 6.

24. Knight, "Sexual Disorientation," 6. See also Dr. Paul Cameron, William I. Playfair, and Stephen Wellum, "The Homosexual Lifespan" (Washington, D.C.: Family Research Institute, 1992).

25. David Horowitz, The "Queer Fellows," _American Spectator_ (January 1993): 46-48.

26. "Homosexuals Headed for Military; Your Action Needed," _Eagle Forum of Alabama Newsletter_ (January/February 1993): 2.

27. "Adopted Resolutions, Jewish War Veterans of the United States" (16-23 August 1992, Baltimore, MD) 8; cited by Robert H. Knight and Daniel S. Garcia, "How Lifting the Military Homosexual Ban May Affect Families" (Family Research Council, Washington D.C., November 1992), 2.

28. Dr. Ann M. Hardy, et al, "The Economic Impact of the First 10,000 Cases of Acquired Immune-deficiency Syndrome in the United States," *Journal of the American Medical Association* 255 (10 January 1986): 210.

29. Major R.D. Adair and Captain Joseph C. Meyers, "Admission of Gays to the Military: A Singularly Intolerant Act," *Parameters: U.S. Army War College Quarterly*, 23 (Spring 1993): 16.

Chapter 6: Issue #3: Pedophilia and Other Crimes

1. Dr. Paul Cameron, et. al., "Child Molestation and Homosexuality," *Psychological Reports* 58 (1986): 327-337.

2. Dr. Charles Davis, Dean of Academic Affairs, Air War College, and Professor of Statistics, Southwest Texas State University; statistical computations explained and verified in telephone conversation 26 January 93.

3. Robert Knight, "Sexual Disorientation: Faulty Research in the Homosexual Debate" (Family Research Council, Washington, D.C., June 1992), 6-7.

4. "No Place for Homo-Homophobia," *Sentinel* (26 March 1992).

5. Dr. Frank du Mas, *Gay Is Not Good* (Nashville: Thomas Nelson, 1980), 255.

6. William H. Masters and Virginia E. Johnson, *Homosexuality in Perspective* (Boston: Little, Brown & Co., 1979), 179-181.

Chapter 7: Issue #4: Security Risks

1. Secretary of Defense Richard Cheney, quoted by Robert Knight, "Sexual Disorientation: Faulty Research in the Homosexual Debate" (Family Research Council, Washington, D.C., June 1992), 2.

2. Knight, "Sexual Disorientation," 2.

3. Major Melissa Wells-Petry, "The Power to Raise and Support Armies: The Homosexual Exclusion Policy in Perspective" (LLM thesis, University of Virginia Judge Advocate General School, 1991, to be published by Gateway-Regnery, May 1993), 86ff.

4. High Tech Gays v Defense Industrial Security Clearance Office, 895 F. 2d. 576 (1990).

5. Wells-Petry, "The Power to Praise and Support Armies," 87-88.

Chapter 8: Issue #5: Heterosexual Privacy

1. Major Melissa Wells-Petry, "The Power to Raise and Support Armies: The Homosexual Exclusion Policy in Perspective" (LLM thesis, University of Virginia Judge Advocate General School, 1991, to be published by Gateway-Regnery, May 1993), 89-90.

2. Ibid., 91-92.

3. General H. Norman Schwarzkopf, Declaration in *Matthews v. Marsh*, Civil Action File No. 82-0216P, U.S. District Court, Maine, 1982; quoted by Lt. Col. Vickie S. Longenecker, "Facts or Fear from the Foxhole" (Military Studies Program paper, U.S. Army War College, Carlisle Barracks, PA, 15 April 1992), 20.

4. Longenecker, "Facts or Fear," 20-21.

5. Steffan v Cheney, 780 F. Supp. 1 (1991).

Chapter 9: Issue #6: Morale and Discipline

1. Lt. Col. John F. Guilmartin quoted by Barry D. Watts, "Toward a Less Mechanistic Image of War," *Air War College Associate Programs Vol. I* (General Purpose Forces-SF 614), 184.

2. Col. David Hackworth, "The Case for a Military Gay Ban," *Washington Post* (28 June 1992): C5.

3. Eldon Yates, quoted in "Coalition to Oppose Gays in Armed Forces," *Washington Times* (2 December 92): 1, 13.

4. S.L.A. Marshall, quoted by Barry Watts, "Toward a Less Mechanistic Image," 187-188.

5. Secretary of Defense Richard Cheney, quoted in "Clinton's First Mistake," *San Diego Union-Tribune* (29 November 1992): C-4, 8.

6. Hackworth, "The Case for a Military Gay Ban."

7. Ibid.

8. Kevin M. McCrane, "Gays in the Military? A Cautionary Tale," *Wall Street Journal* (2 December 1992): A-10.

9. Col. William A. Woodruff, "The Battle Over Homosexuality: Why the Military's Ban Should Not Be Lifted" (Washington, D.C. Family Research Council, December 1992), 4.

10. Mary Newcombe, lecture response to questions at workshop entitled "Excluding Lesbians and Gay Men from Military Service: Whither the Policy, Whither the AALS," Gay and Lesbian Legal Issues Committee, annual meeting of the Association of American Law Schools (AALS), San Francisco, CA, 9 January 1993.

11. Ibid.

12. Gen. Colin L. Powell, quoted by "Powell 'Gays in Military, Farmore Complicated Issue,'" *Air Force Times* (14 December 1992): 12.

Chapter 10: Issue #7: Problems of Implementation

1. Lt. Michael Thomas McIntyre, "Homosexuality and the U.S. Military" (Master thesis, Naval Postgraduate School, Monterey, CA, June 1990), 113-117.

2. "Recommendations for Accepting Homosexuals and Bisexuals into the U.S. Armed Forces," Gay, Lesbian, and Bisexual Military Freedom Project, February 1993.

3. Michael Petrelis,"Homosexuals Headed for Military; Your Action Needed," *Eagle Forum of Alabama Newsletter* (January/February 1993): 2.

Chapter 11: Conclusions and Recommendations

1. U.S. Sen. Daniel Patrick Moynihan, D-NY, "Society's Passiveness Helps Harmful Behavior Spread,"*Omaha World-Herald* (24 January 1993): 17A.

2. Sun Tzu, *The Art of War*, approx. 5th century B.C.

Appendix

1. Lt. Michael Thomas McIntyre, "Homosexuality and the U.S. Military" (Master thesis, Naval Postgraduate School, Monterey, CA, June 1990).

2. Lt. Col. Vickie S. Longenecker, "Facts or Fear from the Foxhole" (Military Studies Program paper, U.S. Army War College, Carlisle Barracks, PA, 15 April 1992), ii.

3. Ibid., 1.

4. Ibid., 10.

5. Ibid., 4.

6. Ibid., 6.

7. Ibid., 22-23, 27-28.

8. Major Billy F. Lacy, "The Homosexual In Uniform" (Research study paper, Air Command and Staff College, Air University, Maxwell AFB, Montgomery, AL, May 1976); Major Dean A. Johnson, "The Homosexual Challenge" (Research study paper, Air Command and Staff College, Air University, Maxwell AFB, Montgomery, AL, May 1976); Capt. James E. Foley, "Updating the Policy Barring Homosexuals from Military Service" (Military essay, Armed Forces Staff College, Norfolk, VA, 9 May 1983).

9. "Defense Force Management: DOD's Policy on Homosexuality" *United States General Accounting Office Report to Congressional Requesters GAO/NS/AD-92-98* (12 June 1992).

10. Major Melissa Wells-Petry, "The Power to Raise and Support Armies: The Homosexual Exclusion Policy in Perspective" (LLM thesis, University of Virginia Judge Advo-

cate General School, 1991; to be published by Gateway-Regnery, May 1993).

11. Commander Eugene T. Gomulka, Deputy Chaplain, U.S. Marine Corps, "Position Paper on the DOD Policy on Homosexuality" (25 July 1992).

12. Robert H. Knight, "Should the Military's Ban on Homosexuals Be Lifted?" (Family Research Council, Washington, D.C. November 1992).

13. Congressman William E. Dannemeyer (R-CA), "Homosexuals in the Military" (Testimony before a Republican Research Committee hearing, 9 December 1992): 14.

14. Dr. Paul Cameron, Dr. Kirk Cameron, and Dr. Kay Proctor, "Effect of Homosexuality upon Public Health and Social Order," *Psychological Reports* 64 (1989): 1167-1179.

15. Dr. Paul Cameron, Dr. Kirk Cameron, and Dr. Kay Proctor, Homosexuals in the Armed Forces," *Psychological Reports* 62 (1988): 211-219.

More Good Books From
Huntington House Publishers

Recent Releases

America: Awaiting the Verdict
by Mike Russell

We are a nation stricken with an infectious disease. The disease is called "her eval"—we are a nation that has denied, rejected, and betrayed our Christian past. The symptoms of the disease are many and multiplying daily. Mike Russell... these concern us Americans to return to the faith of their founding fathers—the faith upon which our law and government rest—or suffer the consequences. To prove that our forebears were in no way attempting to establish a secular state, as contended by secular humanists, the author presents oft-forgotten but crucial evidence to fortify his—and all Christians'—case.

ISBN 1-56384-034-0 $8.99

The Blessings of Liberty
Restoring the City on the Hill
by Charles Heath

The author believes liberalism is destroying our nation. If we continue to do nothing, says Heath, the traditional family values that we cherish and the kind of government envisioned by our founding fathers will cease to exist. Heath presents a coherent case for limited government, decentralized and self-governing communities, and a return to traditional values. Conservatism, he continues, has its premise in the book of Genesis. It is the only viable philosophy capable of addressing and solving today's problems.

ISBN 1-56384-005-7 Trade Paper $8.99

Don't Touch That Dial:
The Impact of the Media on
Children and the Family
by Barbara Hattemer & Robert Showers

Men and women without any stake in the outcome of the war between the pornographers and our families have come to the qualified, professional agreement that media does have an effect on our children—an effect that is devastatingly significant. Highly respected researchers, psychologists, and sociologists join the realm of pediatricians, district attorneys, parents, teachers, pastors and community leaders—who have diligently combined true to the fight against filthy media—and their latest comprehensive critique of the modern media establishment (i.e. film, television, print, art, curriculum).

ISBN 1-56384-032-4 Trade Paper $9.99
ISBN 1-56384-035-9 Hardcover $19.99

MORE GOOD BOOKS FROM
HUNTINGTON HOUSE PUBLISHERS

RECENT RELEASES

America: Awaiting the Verdict
by Mike Fuselier

We are a nation stricken with an infectious disease. The disease is called betrayal—we are a nation that has denied, rejected, and betrayed our Christian past. The symptoms of the disease are many and multiplying daily. Mike Fuselier thus encourages Americans to return to the faith of their founding fathers—the faith upon which our law and government rest—or suffer the consequences. To prove that our forebearers were in no way attempting to establish a secular state, as contended by secular humanists, the author presents oft-forgotten but crucial evidence to fortify his—and all Christians'—case.

ISBN 1-56384-034-0 $5.99

The Blessings of Liberty: Restoring the City on the Hill
by Charles Heath

The author believes Liberalism is destroying our nation. If we continue to do nothing, says Heath, the traditional family values that we cherish and the kind of government envisioned by our founding fathers will cease to exist. Heath presents a coherent case for limited government, decentralized and self-governing communities, and a return to traditional values. Conservatism, he continues, has its premise in the book of Genesis. It is the only viable philosophy capable of addressing and solving today's problems.

ISBN 1-56384-005-7 Trade Paper $8.99

Don't Touch That Dial: The Impact of the Media on Children and the Family
by Barbara Hattemer & Robert Showers

Men and women without any stake in the outcome of the war between the pornographers and our families have come to the qualified, professional agreement that media does have an effect on our children—an effect that is devastatingly significant. Highly respected researchers, psychologists, and sociologists join the realm of pediatricians, district attorneys, parents, teachers, pastors, and community leaders—who have diligently remained true to the fight against filthy media—in their latest comprehensive critique of the modern media establishment (i.e., film, television, print, art, curriculum).

ISBN 1-56384-032-4 Trade Paper $9.99
ISBN 1-56384-035-9 Hardcover $19.99

A Jewish Conservative Looks at Pagan America
by Don Feder

With eloquence and insight that rival contemporary commentators and essayists of antiquity, Don Feder's pen finds his targets in the enemies of God, family, and American tradition and morality. Deftly . . . delightfully . . . the master allegorist and Titian with a typewriter brings clarity to the most complex sociological issues and invokes giggles and wry smiles from both followers and foes. Feder is Jewish to the core, and he finds in his Judaism no inconsistency with an American Judeo-Christian ethic. Questions of morality plague school administrators, district court judges, senators, congressmen, parents, and employers; they are wrestling for answers in a "changing world." Feder challenges this generation and directs inquirers to the original books of wisdom: the Torah and the Bible.

ISBN 1-56384-036-7 Trade Paper $9.99
ISBN 1-56384-037-5 Hardcover $19.99

Journey into Darkness: Nowhere to Land
by Stephen L. Arrington

This story begins on Hawaii's glistening sands and ends in the mysterious deep of the Great White Shark. In between, he found himself trapped in the drug smuggling trade—unwittingly becoming the "Fall Guy" in the highly publicized John Z. DeLorean drug case. Naval career shattered, his youthful innocence tested, and friends and family put to the test of loyalty, Arrington locked on one truth during his savage stay in prison and endeavors to share that critical truth now. Focusing on a single important message to young people—to stay away from drugs—the author recounts his horrifying prison experience and allows the reader to take a peek at the source of hope and courage that helped him survive.

ISBN 1-56384-003-3 $9.99

Political Correctness:
The Cloning of the American Mind
by David Thibodaux, Ph.D.

The author, a professor of literature at the University of Southwestern Louisiana, confronts head on the movement that is now being called Political Correctness. Political correctness, says Thibodaux, "is an umbrella under which advocates of civil rights, gay and lesbian rights, feminism, and environmental causes have gathered." To incur the wrath of these groups, one only has to disagree with them on political, moral, or social issues. To express traditionally Western concepts in universities today can result in not only ostracism, but even suspension. (According to a recent "McNeil-Lehrer News Hour" report, one student was suspended for discussing the reality of the moral law with an avowed homosexual. He was reinstated only after he apologized.)

ISBN 1-56384-026-X Trade Paper $9.99

Subtle Serpent:
New Age in the Classroom

by Darylann Whitemarsh &
Bill Reisman

There is a new morality being taught to our children in public schools. Without the consent or even awareness of parents—educators and social engineers are aggressively introducing new moral codes to our children. In most instances, these new moral codes contradict the traditional values. Darylann Whitemarsh (a 1989 Teacher of the Year recipient) and Bill Reisman (educator and expert on the occult) combine their knowledge to expose the deliberate madness occurring in our public schools.

ISBN 1-56384-016-2 $9.99

When the Wicked Seize a City

by Chuck & Donna McIlhenny with Frank York

A highly publicized lawsuit . . . a house fire-bombed in the night . . . the shatter of windows smashed by politically (and wickedly) motivated vandals cuts into the night. . . . All this because Chuck McIlhenny voiced God's condemnation of a behavior and life-style and protested the destruction of society that results from its practice. That behavior is homosexuality, and that life-style is the gay culture. This book explores: the rise of gay power and what it will mean if Christians do not organize and prepare for the battle; homosexual attempts to have the American Psychiatric Association remove pedophilia from the list of mental illnesses—now they want homophobia declared a disorder.

ISBN 1-56384-024-3 $9.99

You Hit Like a Girl

by Elsa Houtz & William J. Ferkile

Rape—it's the issue that dominates the headlines. Have things changed since the days when women and children were afforded respect and care by all members of society? What does self-protection mean in the 1990s in this age of higher rates of violent crime and the "progressiveness" of the women's movement? What can women do to protect themselves? What can men do to protect the women they love—or the children they'd sacrifice their very lives to shelter from harm? The authors, self-defense experts, have developed a thorough guide to self-protection that addresses the mental attitude of common sense safety and details the practical means by which women can protect themselves and their children.

ISBN 1-56384-031-6 $9.99

BACKLIST/BEST-SELLERS

Deadly Deception
by Jim Shaw & Tom McKinney

For the first time the 33 degree ritual is made public! Learn of the "secrets" and "deceptions" that are practiced daily around the world. Find out why Freemasonry teaches that it is the true religion, that all other religions are only corrupted and perverted forms of Freemasonry. If you know anyone in the Masonic movement, you must read this book.

ISBN 0-910311-54-4 $7.99

Exposing the AIDS Scandal
by Dr. Paul Cameron

Where do you turn when those who control the flow of information in this country withhold the truth? Why is the national media hiding facts from the public? Can AIDS be spread in ways we're not being told? Finally, a book that gives you a total account for the AIDS epidemic, and what steps can be taken to protect yourself. What you don't know can kill you!

ISBN 0-910311-52-8 $7.99

Hidden Dangers of the Rainbow
by Constance Cumbey

The first book to uncover and expose the New Age movement, this national #1 best-seller paved the way for all other books on the subject. It has become a giant in its category. This book provides the vivid exposé of the New Age movement, which the author contends is dedicated to wiping out Christianity and establishing a one world order. This movement, a vast network of occult and pagan organizations, meets the tests of prophecy concerning the Antichrist.

ISBN 0-910311-03-X $8.99

Kinsey, Sex and Fraud:
The Indoctrination of a People
by Dr. Judith A. Reisman and Edward Eichel

Kinsey, Sex and Fraud describes the research of Alfred Kinsey which shaped Western society's beliefs and understanding of the nature of human sexuality. His unchallenged conclusions are taught at every level of education—elementary, high school and college—and quoted in textbooks as undisputed truth.

The authors clearly demonstrate that Kinsey's research involved illegal experimentations on several hundred children. The survey was carried out on a non-representative group of Americans, including disproportionately large numbers of sex offenders, prostitutes, prison inmates and exhibitionists.

ISBN 0-910311-20-X Hardcover $19.95

New World Order:
The Ancient Plan of Secret Societies
by William T. Still

For thousands of years, secret societies have cultivated an ancient plan which has powerfully influenced world events. Until now, this secret plan has remained hidden from view. This book presents new evidence that a military take-over of the U.S. was considered by some in the administration of one of our recent presidents. Although averted, the forces behind it remain in secretive positions of power.

ISBN 0-910311-64-1 $8.99

"Soft Porn" Plays Hardball
by Dr. Judith A. Reisman

With amazing clarity, the author demonstrates that pornography imposes on society a view of women and children that encourages violence and sexual abuse. As crimes against women and children increase to alarming proportions, it's of paramount importance that we recognize the cause of this violence. Pornography should be held accountable for the havoc it has wreaked in our homes and our country.

ISBN 0-910311-65-X Trade Paper $8.99
ISBN 0-910311-92-7 Hardcover $16.95